Ordnance Survey

G000096084

Derby
and Belper

Allestree · Alvaston · Borrowash · Chaddesden
Duffield · Little Eaton · Littleover · Mickleover

STREET ATLAS

Contents

II Key to map symbols
III Key to map pages
IV Route planning
1 Street maps
20 Index of hospitals, railway stations, schools, shopping centres, street names and universities

PHILIP'S

First edition published 1998 by
Ordnance Survey®
Romsey Road, Maybush,
Southampton SO16 4GU
and
George Philip Ltd
an imprint of Reed Consumer Books Ltd
Michelin House, 81 Fulham Road, London
SW3 6RB and Auckland, Melbourne

ISBN 0-540-07608-2

The mapping between pages 1 and 19 in this atlas is derived from Ordnance Survey® Large Scale and Landranger® mapping and revised using Ordnance Survey® Land-line® data.

Ordnance Survey, Land-Line and Landranger are registered trade marks of Ordnance Survey, the National Mapping Agency of Great Britain.

Printed and bound in Spain by Cayfosa

22a	**Motorway** (with junction number)
	Primary route (dual carriageway and single)
	A road (dual carriageway and single)
	B road (dual carriageway and single)
	Minor road (dual carriageway and single)
	Other minor road
	Road under construction
	Pedestrianised area
	County and Unitary Authority boundaries
	Railway
	Tramway, miniature railway
	Rural track, private road or narrow road in urban area
	Gate or obstruction to traffic (restrictions may not apply at all times or to all vehicles)
	Path, bridleway, byway open to all traffic, road used as a public path

The representation in this atlas of a road, track or path is no evidence of the existence of a right of way

23

12

Adjoining page indicators

	British Rail station
M	**Metrolink station**
	Underground station
D	**Docklands Light Railway station**
M	**Tyne and Wear Metro**
	Private railway station
	Bus, coach station
◆	**Ambulance station**
◆	**Coastguard station**
◆	**Fire station**
◆	**Police station**
✚	**Accident and Emergency entrance to hospital**
H	**Hospital**
✝	**Church, place of worship**
i	**Information centre** (open all year)
P P&R	**Parking, Park and Ride**
PO	**Post Office**
Prim Sch	**Important buildings, schools, colleges, universities and hospitals**
River Medway	**Water name**
	Stream
	River or canal (minor and major)
	Water
	Tidal water
	Woods
	Houses
House	**Non-Roman antiquity**
VILLA	**Roman antiquity**

Acad	**Academy**	Mon	**Monument**
Cemy	**Cemetery**	Mus	**Museum**
C Ctr	**Civic Centre**	Obsy	**Observatory**
CH	**Club House**	Pal	**Royal Palace**
Coll	**College**	PH	**Public House**
Ent	**Enterprise**	Recn Gd	**Recreation Ground**
Ex H	**Exhibition Hall**	Resr	**Reservoir**
Ind Est	**Industrial Estate**	Ret Pk	**Retail Park**
Inst	**Institute**	Sch	**School**
Ct	**Law Court**	Sh Ctr	**Shopping Centre**
L Ctr	**Leisure Centre**	Sta	**Station**
LC	**Level Crossing**	TH	**Town Hall/House**
Liby	**Library**	Trad Est	**Trading Estate**
Mkt	**Market**	Univ	**University**
Meml	**Memorial**	YH	**Youth Hostel**

■ The dark grey border on the inside edge of some pages indicates that the mapping does not continue onto the adjacent page

■ The small numbers around the edges of the maps identify the 1 kilometre National Grid lines

The scale of the maps is 6.13 cm to 1 km (3⁷/₈ inches to 1 mile)

0	¼	½	¾	1 mile
0	250m	500m	750m	1 kilometre

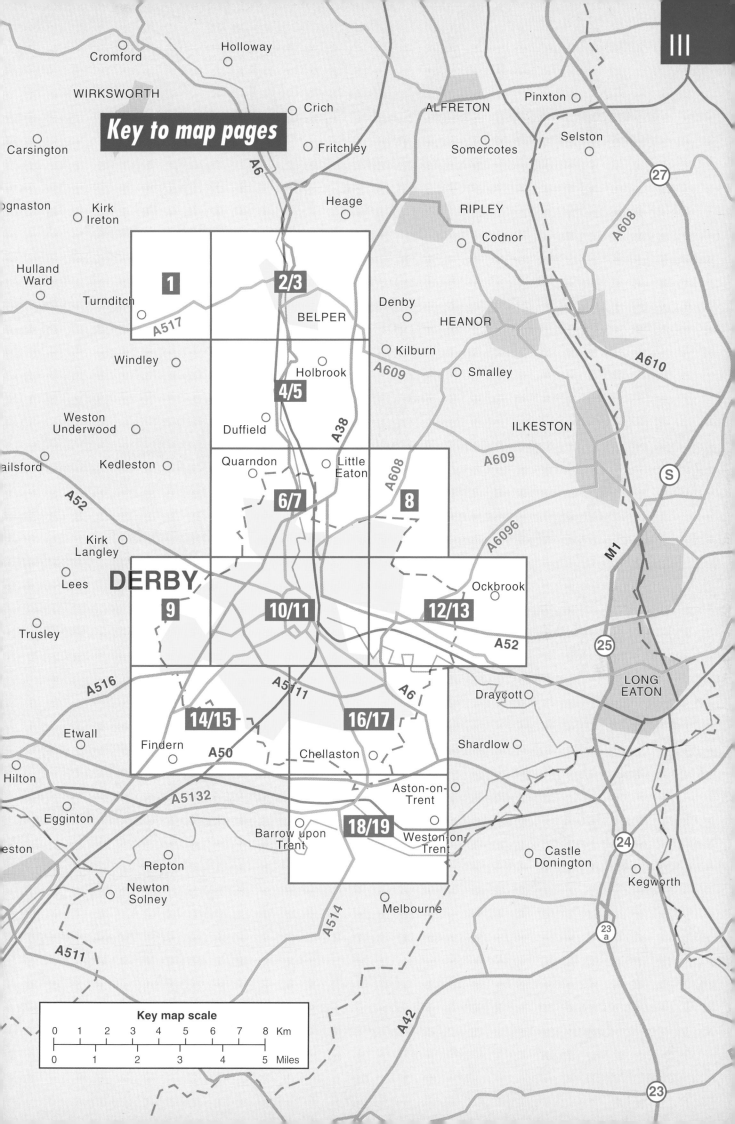

Key to map pages

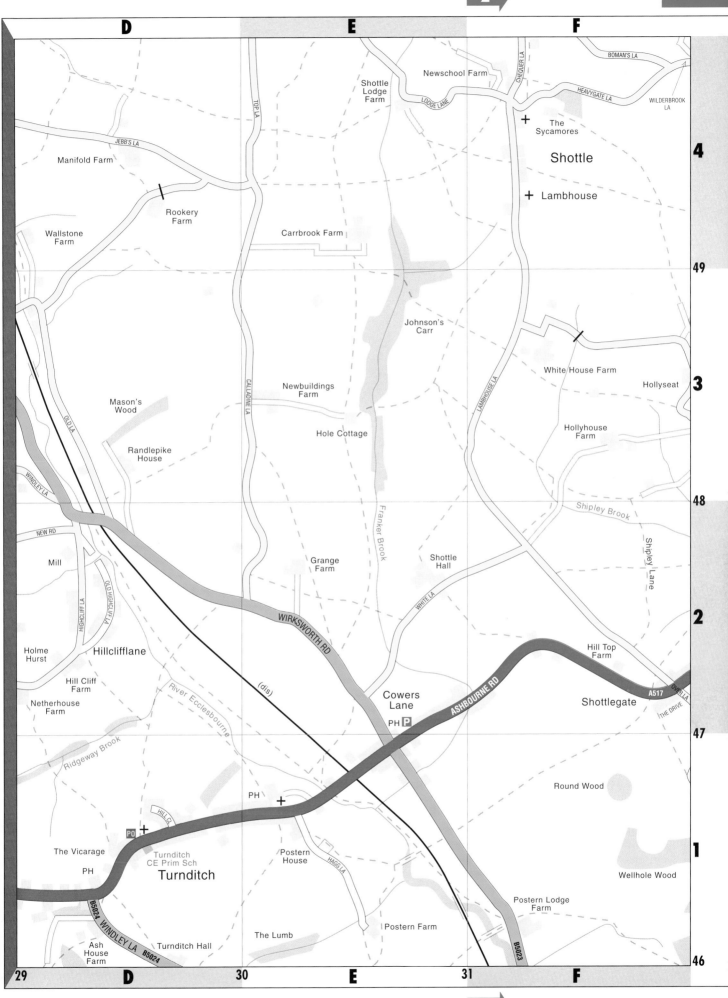

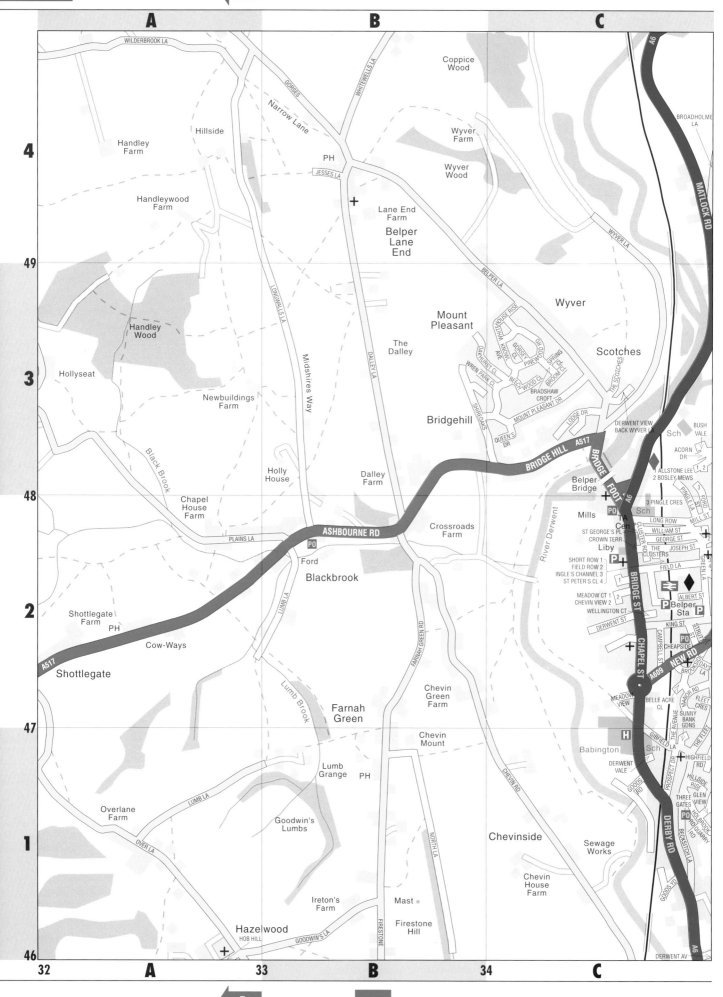

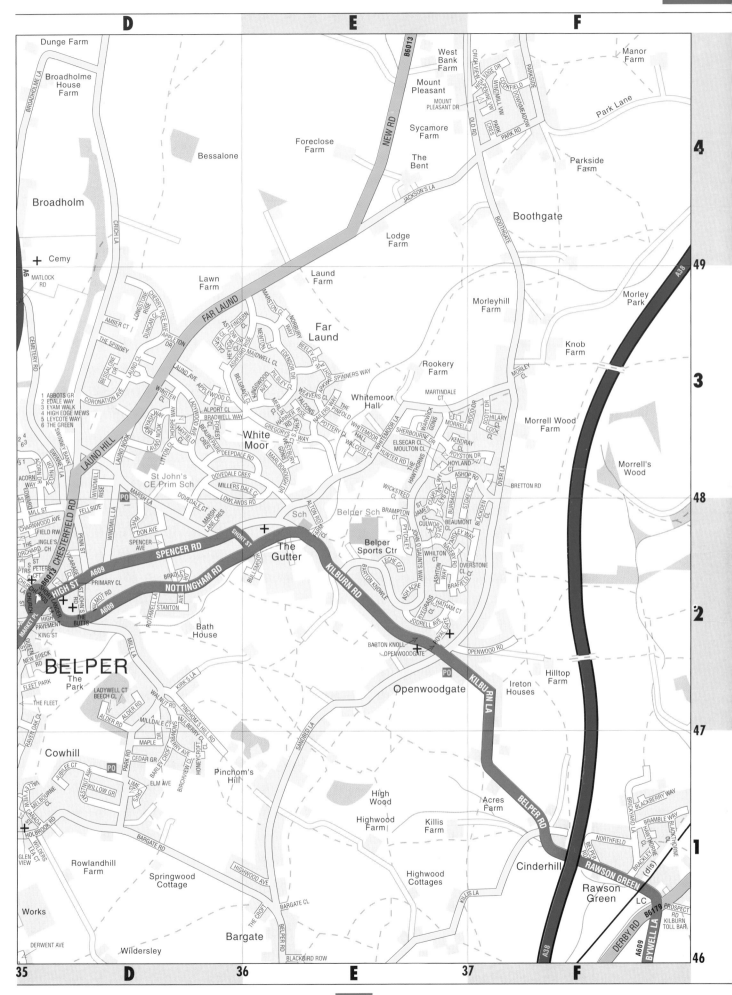

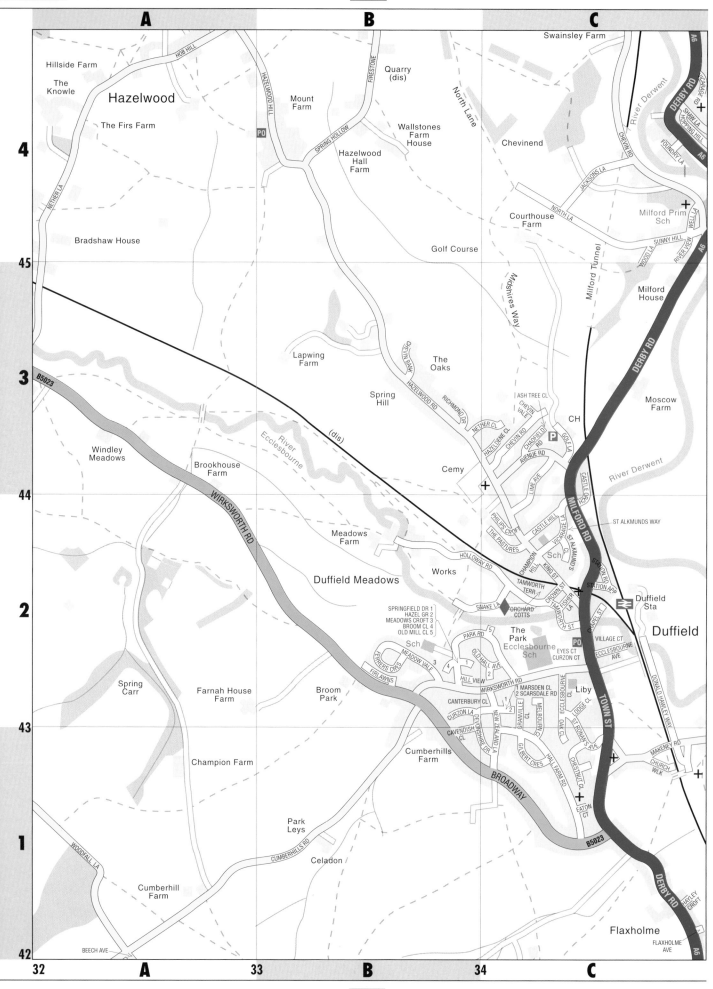

A **B** **C**

Swainsley Farm

Hillside Farm

The Knowle

Hazelwood

Mount Farm

Quarry (dis)

FIRESTONE

HAZELWOOD HILL

North Lane

Chevinend

River Derwent

DERBY RD

A6

VICARAGE RD

SHAW LA

HOPPING HILL

FOUNDRY LA

A6

The Firs Farm

PO

SPRING HOLLOW

Wallstones Farm House

Hazelwood Hall Farm

JACKSONS LA

NORTH LA

Milford Prim Sch

WELL LA

RIVER VIEW

SUNNY HILL

WOOD LA

Bradshaw House

NETHER LA

Courthouse Farm

Golf Course

Milford Tunnel

Milford House

4

45

Midshires Way

Lapwing Farm

The Oaks

CHEVIN BANK

HAZELWOOD RD

RICHMOND DR

ASH TREE CL

CHEVIN VALE

Moscow Farm

3

B5023

Spring Hill

NETHER CL

HAZELDENE CL

CHEVIN RD

CHADFIELD RD

CH

DERBY RD

River Ecclesbourne

(dis)

AVENUE RD

GOLF LA

P

CASTLE HILL

CASTLE ORCH

River Derwent

Windley Meadows

Brookhouse Farm

WIRKSWORTH RD

Cemy

LIME AVE

PHILLIPS CROFT

St Alkmunds Way

44

Meadows Farm

HOLLOWAY RD

Works

THE PASTURES

CHAMPION HILL

CASTLE HILL

VICARAGE RD

ST ALKMUNDS

Sch

MILFORD RD

KING ST

FISHER LA

STATION APP

Duffield Sta

St ALKMUNDS WAY

Duffield Meadows

SNAKE LA

ORCHARD COTTS

CROWN ST

TAMWORTH TERR

TAMWORTH ST

CHAPEL ST

Duffield

2

SPRINGFIELD DR 1
HAZEL GR 2
MEADOWS CROFT 3
BROOM CL 4
OLD MILL CL 5

PARK RD

The Park

Ecclesbourne Sch

PO

VILLAGE CT

EYES CT

CURZON CT

ECCLESBOURNE AVE

Spring Carr

Farnah House Farm

Broom Park

FERRERS CRES

MEADOW VALE

Sch

FIRLAWNS

OLD HALL AVE

HILL VIEW

WIRKSWORTH RD

CANTERBURY CL

MARSDEN CL 1
SCARSDALE RD 2

MELBOURN CL

ECCLESBOURNE CL

LODGE CL

Liby

TOWN ST

CURZON LA

DEVONSHIRE DR

NEW ZEALAND LA

GRANVILLE CL

OAK CL

St RONANS AVE

MAKENEY RD

DONALD HAWLEY WAY

43

Champion Farm

CAVENDISH CL

GILBERT CRES

HALL FARM RD

CHESTNUT CL

CHURCH WLK

Cumberhills Farm

BROADWAY

EATON CT

1

WOODFALL LA

Park Leys

CUMBERHILLS RD

Celadon

B5023

DERBY RD

A6

Flaxholme

FLAXHOLME AVE

HAVLEY CROFT

42

BEECH AVE

32 **A** **33** **B** **34** **C**

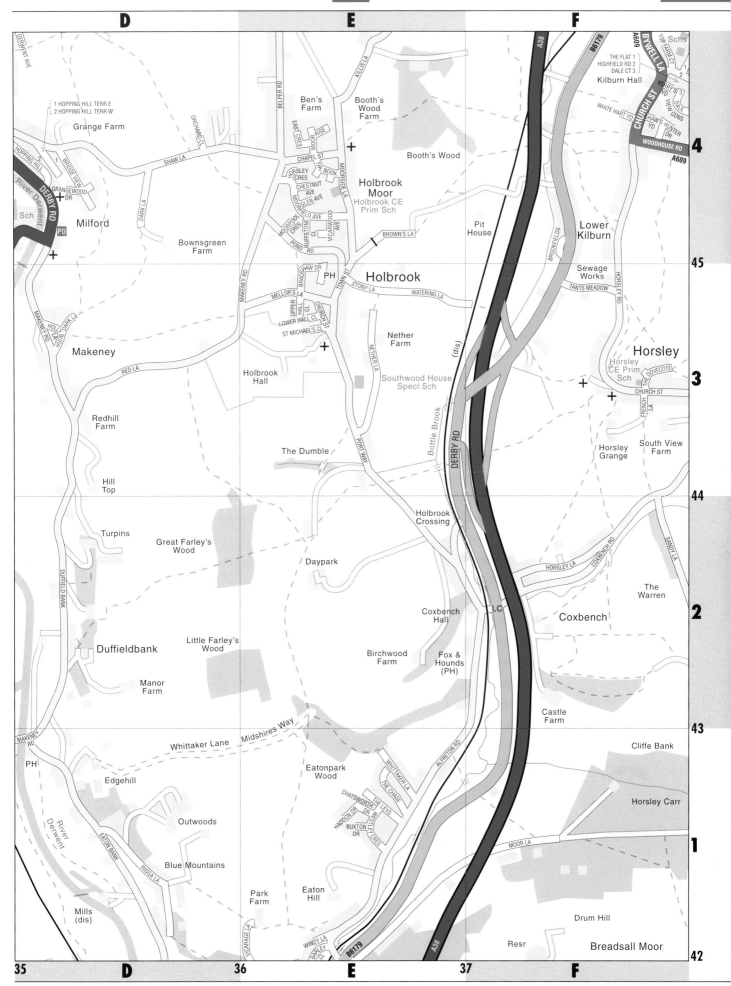

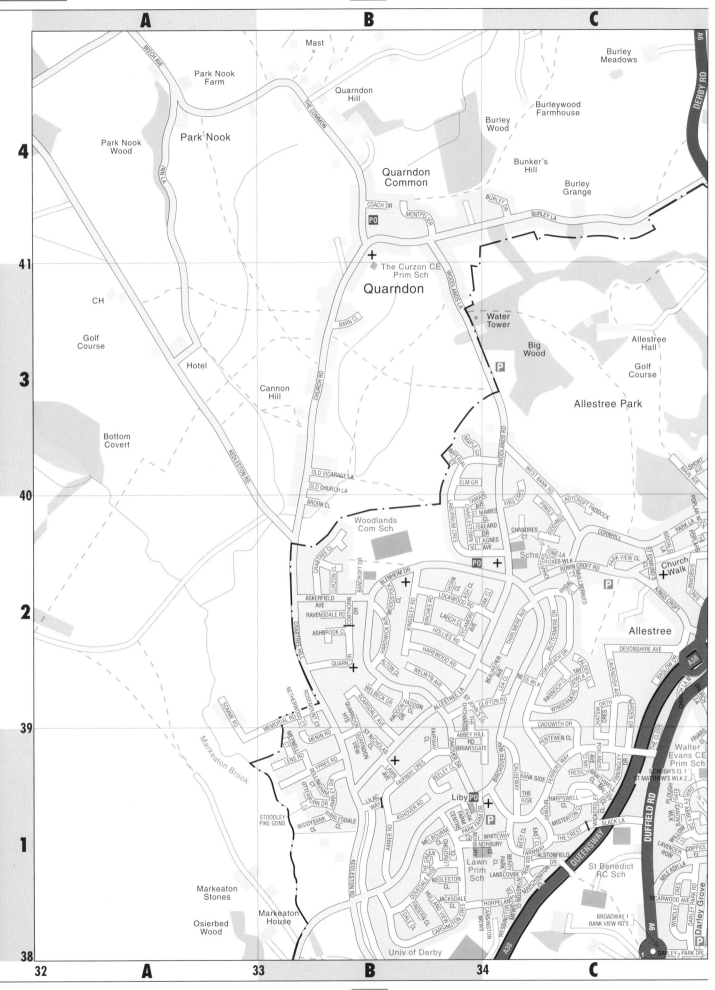

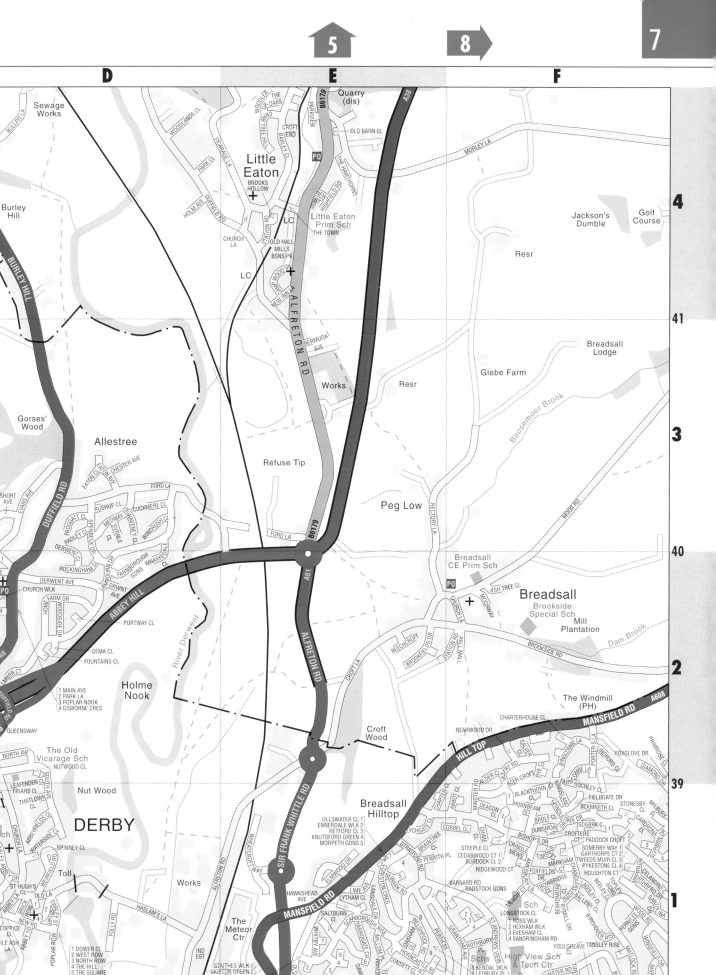

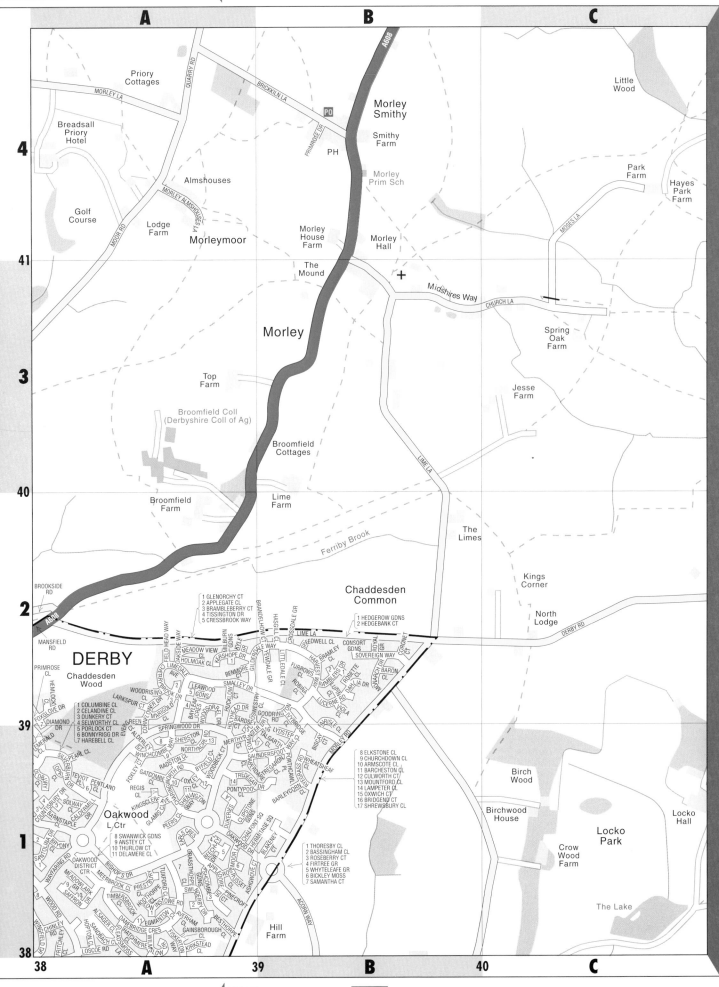

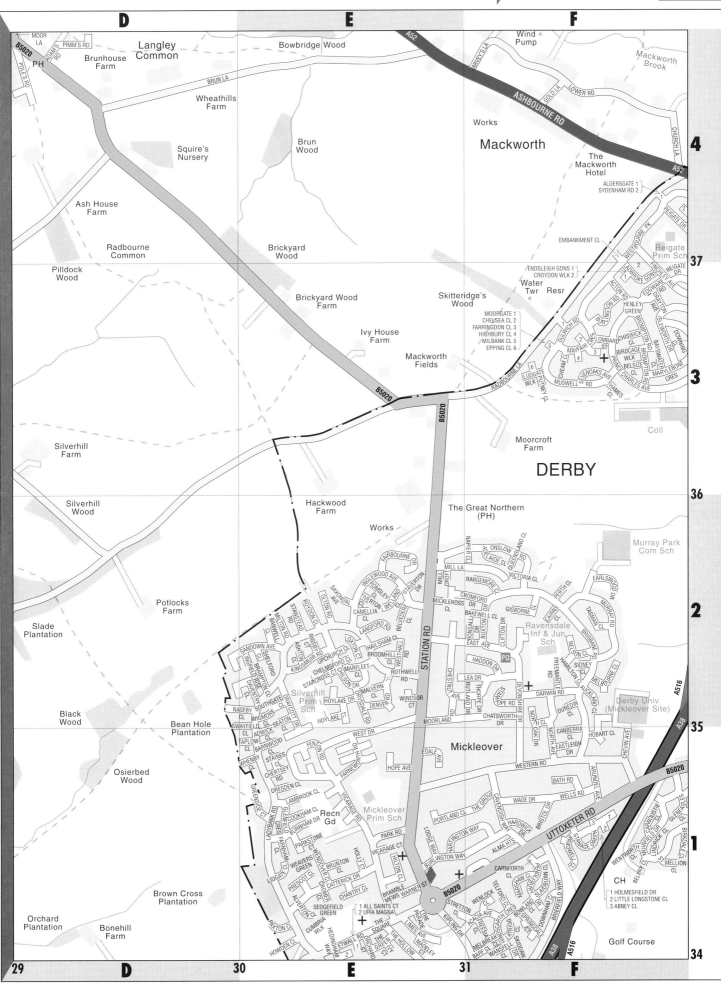

D   E   F

MOOR LA
B5020
PIMM'S RD
ADAM'S RD
POLES RD
PH

Langley Common
Bowbridge Wood

A52

Wind Pump
Mackworth Brook

Brunhouse Farm
BRUN LA
Wheathills Farm

ASHBOURNE RD
GOLD LA
LOWER RD
CHURCH LA

Squire's Nursery
Brun Wood

Works

Mackworth
4

The Mackworth Hotel

ALDERSGATE 1
SYDENHAM RD 2

Ash House Farm

Radbourne Common
Brickyard Wood

EMBANKMENT CL

Pilldock Wood

Brickyard Wood Farm

Skitteridge's Wood

ENDSLEIGH GDNS 1
CROYDON WLK 2

Water Twr Resr

WESTBOURNE PK
REIGATE DR
Reigate Prim Sch
37

Ivy House Farm

Mackworth Fields

B5020

MOORGATE 1
CHELSEA CL 2
FARRINGDON CL 3
HIGHBURY CL 4
MILBANK CL 5
EPPING CL 6

LADBROKE GDNS
FINCHLEY RD
DULWICH RD
BURLINGTON RD
ACTON RD
EDGWARE AVE
BRIXTON AVE
ISLEWORTH AVE
DOWNING RD
DRAYTON AVE
BROMPTON RD
BAYSWATER
CHISWICK CL
Henley Green

DERBY

Moorcroft Farm

LOMBARD ST
MAYFAIR CL
CHEAM CL
BIRDCAGE WLK
MUSWELL
SEVENOAKS AVE
PUTNEY CL
RADBOURNE LA
LUDGATE WLK
PRINCE CHARLES AVE
BELSIZE CL
THAMES CL
MARYLEBONE CRES
3

Silverhill Farm

Coll

36

Silverhill Wood

Hackwood Farm

The Great Northern (PH)

Works

Murray Park Com Sch

Potlocks Farm

FAIRBOURNE DR
INGLEWOOD AVE
ROMSLEY CL
TIVERTON CL
CAMELLIA
SAXONDAL
OLTON RD
BELVEDERE CL
STAVERTON DR
WELLAND
NAPIER CL
MILL LA
MILL CROFT
ONSLOW CL
ADELAIDE CL
QUEENSLAND CL
RANGEMORE CL
VICTORIA CL
CROMFORD DR
MICKLEROSS CL
BAKEWELL CL
BUXTON CL
CLIFTON DR
GISBORNE
PERTH CL
CAIRN
EARLSWOOD DR
BRISBANE RD
TASMAN CL
MURRAY RD

Slade Plantation

MILTON RD
STANSTEAD
FOXDON CL
RIGSBY CT
ASHTON CL
KINGSMUIR RD
LOXTON CL
UPCHURCH CL
HAILSHAM CL
BROOMHILL
WESTHALL
ROTHWELL RD
STATION RD
EAST AVE
HADDON DR
PO
LEA DR
THORPE DR
RUTLAND RD
NELSON CL
FREEMANTLE RD
SIDNEY
HAMILTON CL
AUCKLAND RD
MELBO
2

Black Wood

SANDOWN AVE
BANWELL
SHELFORD CL
BRAMPTON CL
LINGFIELD RISE
DAVENTRY
CHELMSFORD CT
STARCROSS CT
CHILSON DR
MARFLEET
MALVERN CL
DENVER
WINDSOR CT
MOORLAND
CHESTNUT
SPE RD
ROPE RD
CHATSWORTH CL
DARWIN RD
DEVONSHIRE DR
NORTH OAK DR
NORTH AVE
DUNEDIN CL
CANBERRA CL
EASTLEIGH DR
HOBART CL
CHEVIN AVE

Derby Univ (Mickleover Site)

Ravensdale Inf & Jun Sch

Bean Hole Plantation

NASEBY
SOUTHGATE
WIGMORE
SWAYFIELD CL
ADWICK CL
BARNWOOD
SEATON CL
Silverhill Prim Sch
HOYLAKE AVE
DRYSDALE RD
HOYLAKE CT
WEST DR
35

Osierbed Wood

WHENBY CL
STAINES CL
CHERTSEY RD
DRESDEN CL
LAMBROOK CL
FENTON RD
FARNEWAY
HOPE AVE
EDALE AVE

Mickleover

WESTERN RD

A516
A38
B5020

UTTOXETER RD

GREENSIDE
LADYRAYNE RD
GLENFIELD
CLEVELAND
COOKHAM CL
BURNHAM DR
Recn Gd
VICARAGE RD
Mickleover Prim Sch
PARK RD
PORTLAND CL
THE GROVE
CAVENDISH WAY
WADE DR
WELLS DR
HARTINGTON WAY
BATH RD
HARDWICK DR
BRISTOL DR
ARUNDEL AVE

Brown Cross Plantation

WEAVERS GREEN
BRUNTON CL
HOLLY CL
HILTON CL
LODGE WAY
BURLWGTON WAY
ALMA HTS
CAVENDISH WAY
WENTWORTH
BELFRY CL
MUIRFIELD DR
CARNOUSTIE
LINDRICK CL
GLENEAGLES
BIRKDALE CL
MELLION
CH
1

Orchard Plantation

LUDGATE
PRESCOT CL
CROMER CL
CATTERICK DR
CHANTRY CL
SEDGEFIELD GREEN
CUMBRIA WLK
ALVERTON CL
BRAMBLE MEWS
WARNER ST
B5020
STRETTON
WENLOCK CL
CARNFORTH CL
TELFORD CL
MARLOW DR
SLADBURN CL
BOWLAND CL
DOWNHAM CL
BRIERFIELD WAY

1 HOLMESFIELD DR
2 LITTLE LONGSTONE CL
3 ABNEY CL

Bonehill Farm

PAXTON CL
HOWDEN CL
HEDINGHAM WAY
ETWALL RD
THE SQUARE
THE PARADE
THE GREEN
THE HOLLOW
LIMES AVE
MADELEY
KIPLING DR
ACACIA AVE
GREENWAY
BARF CL
WANSFELL
SKYDOWN

1 ALL SAINTS CT
UFFA MAGNA
MELBREAK
MAYFIELD
BARF CL
SWALE
CLEE
HAWNBY
SPRINGDALE
WARSCARTH CRES

Golf Course

34

29   D   30   E   31   F

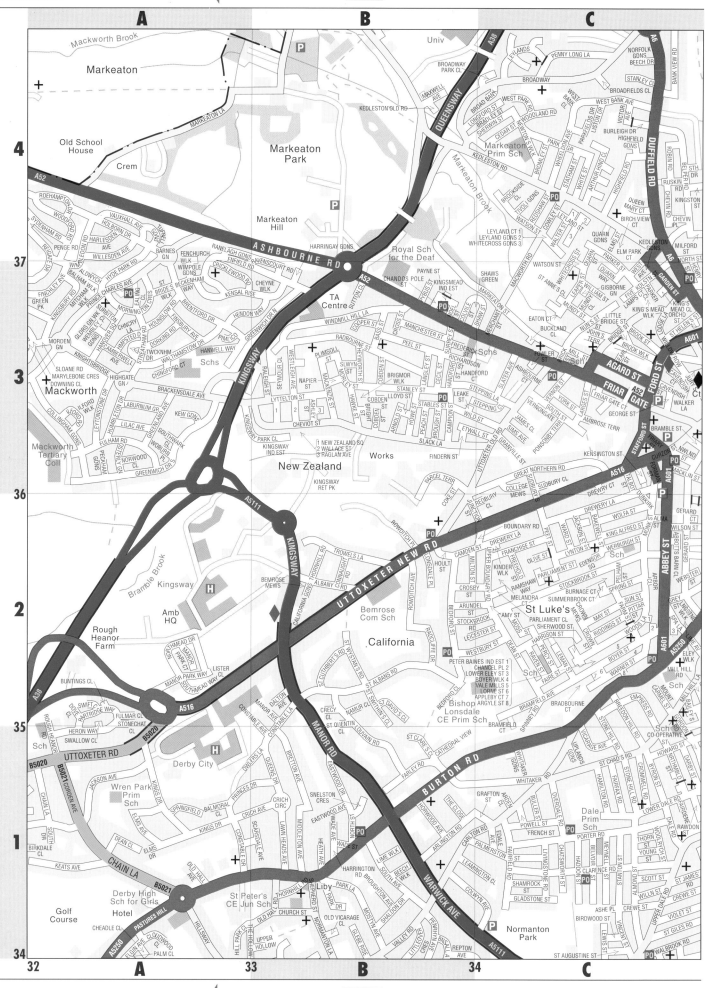

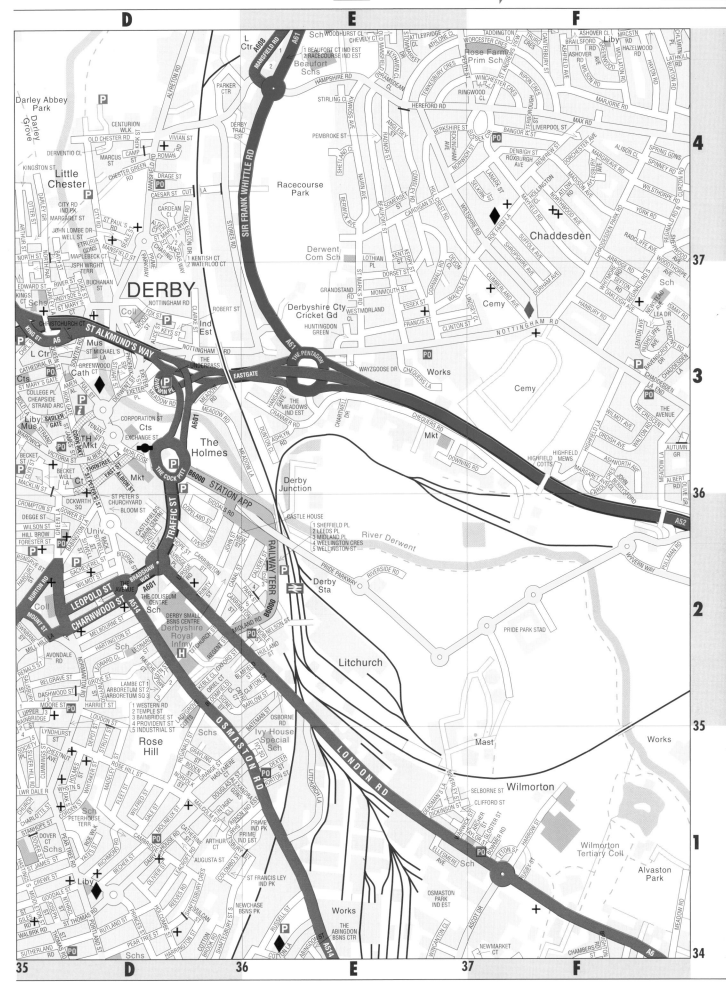

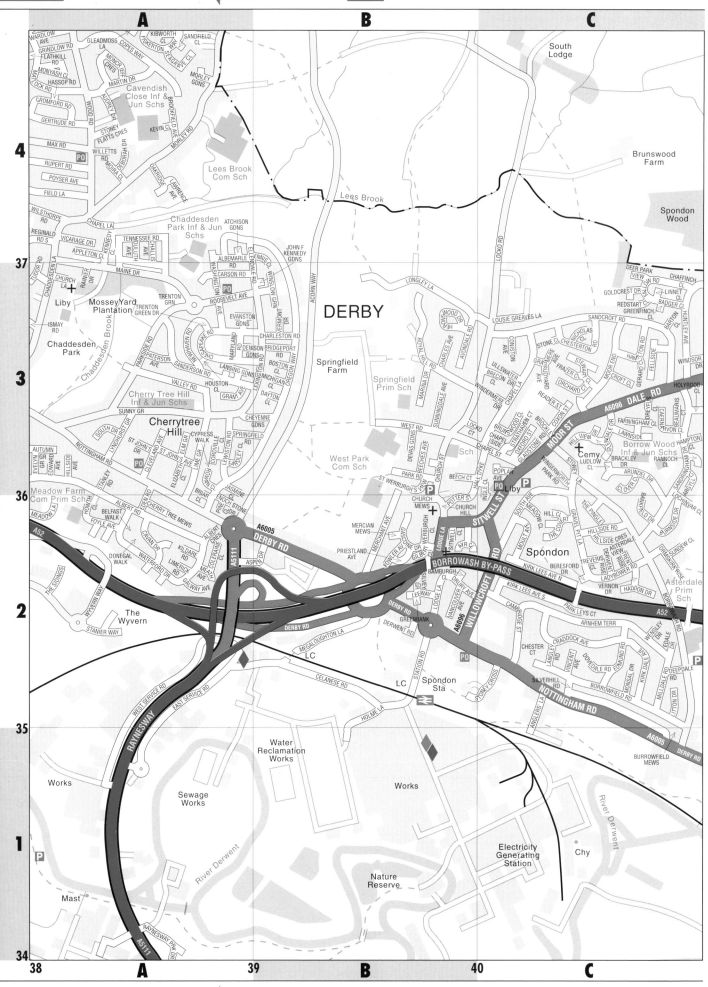

A   **B**   **C**

DERBY

South Lodge

Brunswood Farm

Spondon Wood

Cavendish Close Inf & Jun Schs

Lees Brook Com Sch

Lees Brook

Chaddesden Park Inf & Jun Schs

Deer Park

Mossey Yard Plantation

Liby

Chaddesden Park

Springfield Farm

Springfield Prim Sch

Borrow Wood Inf & Jun Schs

Cherry Tree Hill Inf & Jun Schs

Cherrytree Hill

West Park Com Sch

Spondon

Asterdale Prim Sch

Meadow Farm Com Prim Sch

A6005 DERBY RD

BORROWASH BY-PASS

The Wyvern

Water Reclamation Works

Sewage Works

Spondon Sta

Works

Electricity Generating Station

River Derwent

Nature Reserve

Chy

Works

Mast

RAYNESWAY

NOTTINGHAM RD

WILLOWCROFT RD

SITWELL ST

MOOR ST

A6096 DALE RD

Burrowfield Mews

A6005 DERBY RD

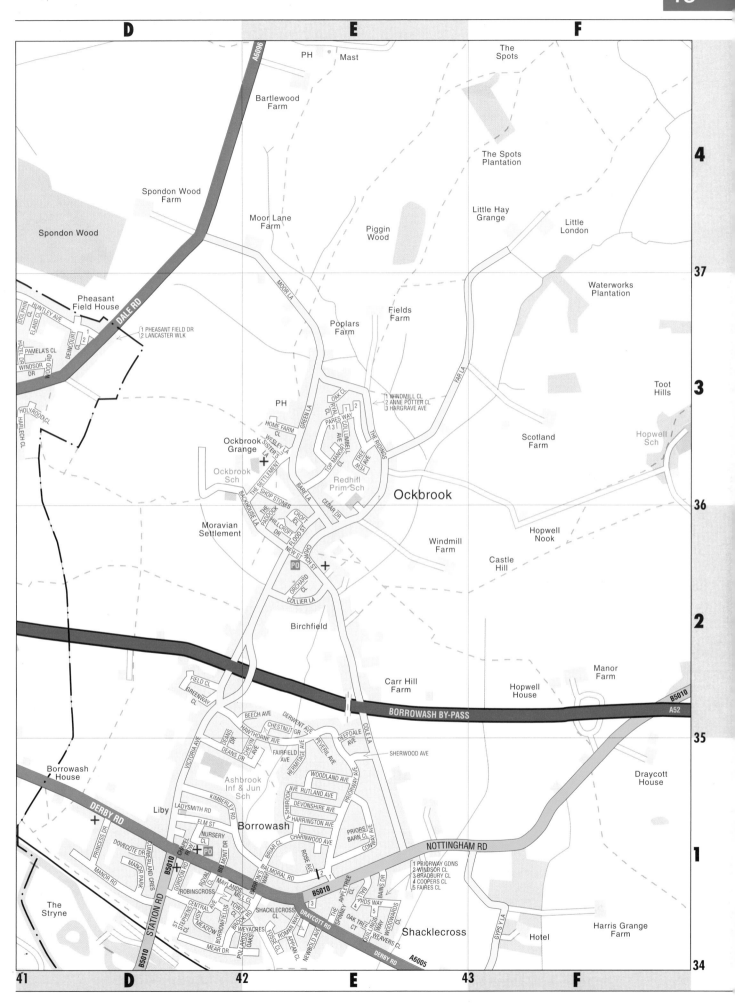

D E F

1 PHEASANT FIELD DR
2 LANCASTER WLK

1 WINDMILL CL
2 ANNE POTTER CL
3 HARGRAVE AVE

1 PRIORWAY GDNS
2 WINDSOR CL
3 BRADBURY CL
4 COOPERS CL
5 FAIRES CL

The Spots

Mast

PH

Bartlewood
Farm

The Spots
Plantation

Spondon Wood
Farm

Little Hay
Grange

Little
London

Moor Lane
Farm

Piggin
Wood

Spondon Wood

Waterworks
Plantation

Pheasant
Field House

Fields
Farm

Poplars
Farm

Toot
Hills

PH

Scotland
Farm

Hopwell
Sch

Ockbrook
Grange

Ockbrook

Ockbrook
Sch

Redhill
Prim Sch

Moravian
Settlement

Hopwell
Nook

Windmill
Farm

Castle
Hill

PO

Birchfield

Manor
Farm

Carr Hill
Farm

Hopwell
House

BORROWASH BY-PASS

B5010

A52

Borrowash
House

Draycott
House

DERBY RD

Liby

Ashbrook
Inf & Jun
Sch

Borrowash

NOTTINGHAM RD

PO

The
Stryne

Shacklecross

Hotel

Harris Grange
Farm

DERBY RD

A6005

41 D 42 E 43 F

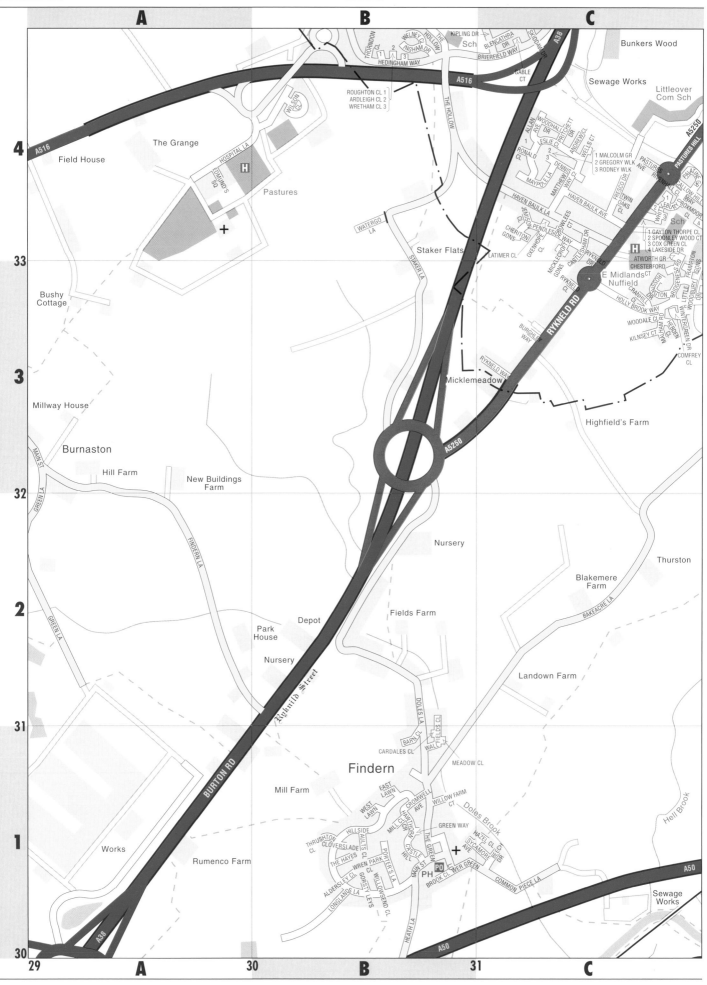

9

A B C

4 A516 Field House The Grange Pastures H EDMUND'S SQ HOSPITAL LA WILSON CL

WELNEY INGHAM DR THE HOLLOW THORNDON CL 1 2 3 HEDINGHAM WAY

ROUGHTON CL 1 ARDLEIGH CL 2 WRETHAM CL 3

A516

KIPLING DR Sch WELNEY BLENCATHRA DR SKIDDAW DR BRIERFIELD WAY Bunkers Wood

GABLE CT Sewage Works Littleover Com Sch

A38 A5250 PASTURES HILL

ALLAN AVE WOODHALL DR PRITCHETT DR ANDREW CL WELLS CT RONALD CL LESLIE CL MATTHEW WAY CT DENNIS WAY MAYPOLE LA FRESCOT DR TWIN OAKS CL

1 MALCOLM GR 2 GREGORY WLK 3 RODNEY WLK PASTURES AVE RIVENHALL CL FALLOW DR PAULINE CT BOXMOOR CL

HAVEN BAULK LA HAVEN BAULK AVE CHERITON GDNS OXENHOPE CT PENDLESIDE WAY JEMISON CT DOWLERS CL CASTLEDALE CT CASTLESHAW DR RYKNELD CL Sch EBURY

1 GAYTON THORPE CL 2 SPOONLEY WOOD CT 3 COX GREEN CL 4 LAKESIDE DR WHITE CL ATWORTH GR CHESTERFORD

33 Bushy Cottage Staker Flats WATERGO LA STAKER LA LATIMER CL

MICKLEOVER GDNS RYKNELD CT RYKNELD DR H E Midlands Nuffield CRANHILL WINTERGREEN DR HOLLY BROOK WAY WOODALE CL MAW HAM RD KILNSEY CT HEBDEN BRIDGNESS RD LITTLE WOODBURY GDNS FRAMPTON CT WOODBURY CL COMFREY CL

BURGHLEY WAY RYKNELD RD

3 Millway House

Burnaston Hill Farm GREEN LA MAIN ST New Buildings Farm FINDERN LA RYKNELD WAY Micklemeadow A5250 Highfield's Farm

32

2 GREEN LA Park House Depot Nursery Highfild Street Fields Farm Nursery Blakemere Farm BAKEACRE LA Thurston Landown Farm

31 BURTON RD DOLES LA FIELDS CL WALL CL BARN CL CARDALES CL MEADOW CL

Findern Mill Farm EAST LAWN WEST LAWN MILL CL GR HAWTHORN CL CROMWELL AVE WILLOW FARM CT GREEN WAY THE GREEN CASTLE HILL MAIN ST Doles Brook HAZEL CL BIRCH CL SYCAMORE AVE Hell Brook

1 Works THRUSHTON CL HILLSIDE CLOVERSLADE THE HAYES AULT'S CL PORTER'S LA WREN PARK CL ALDERSLEY CL GORSTY LEYS WILLOWSEND CL LONGLANDS LA Rumenco Farm BROOK CL GREEN PO PH WER GREEN COMMON PIECE LA HEATH LA A50 Sewage Works

30 A38 A50 A50

29 A 30 B 31 C

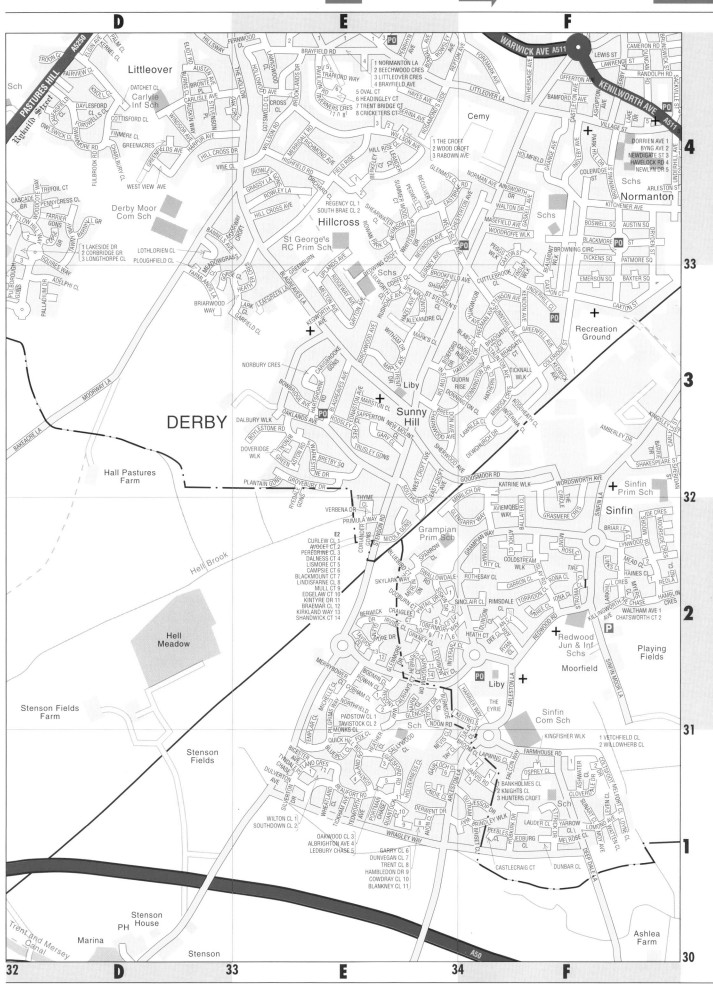

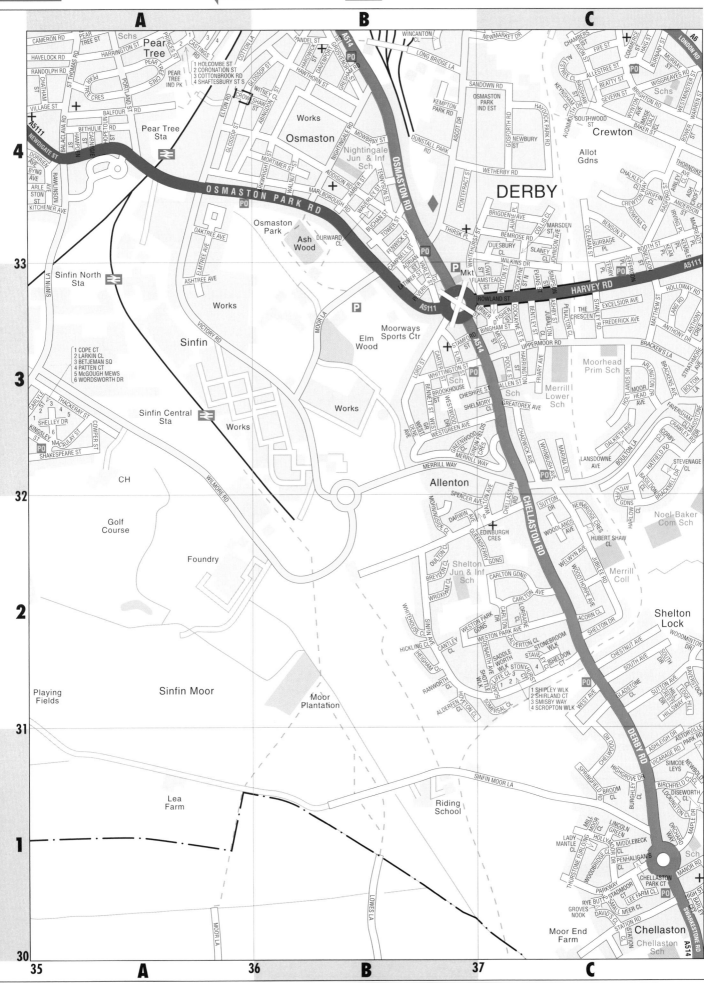

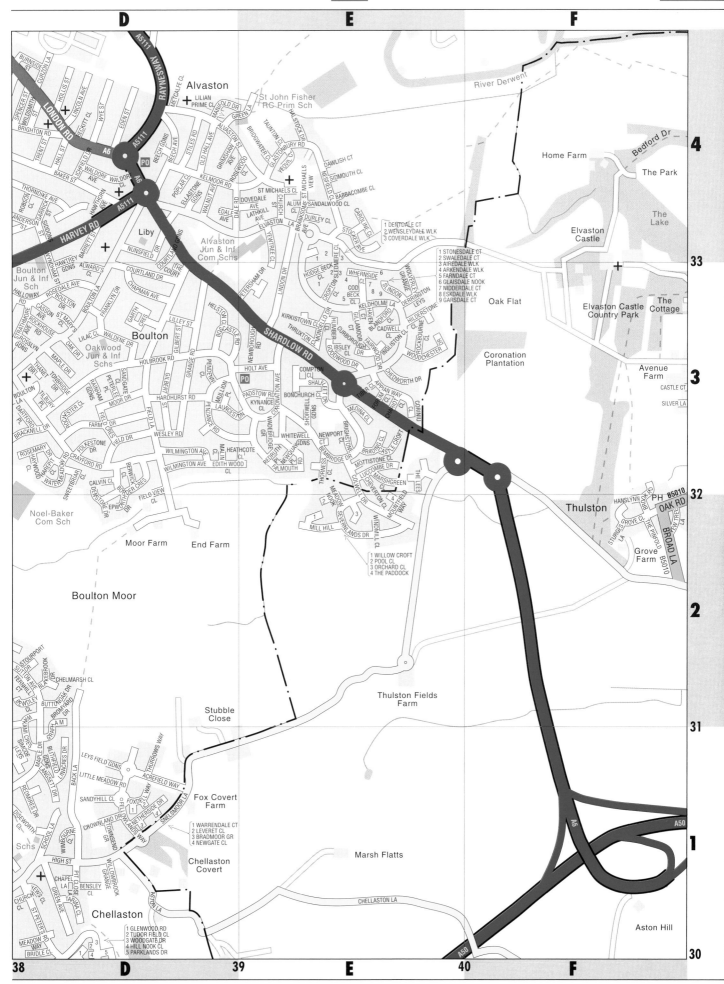

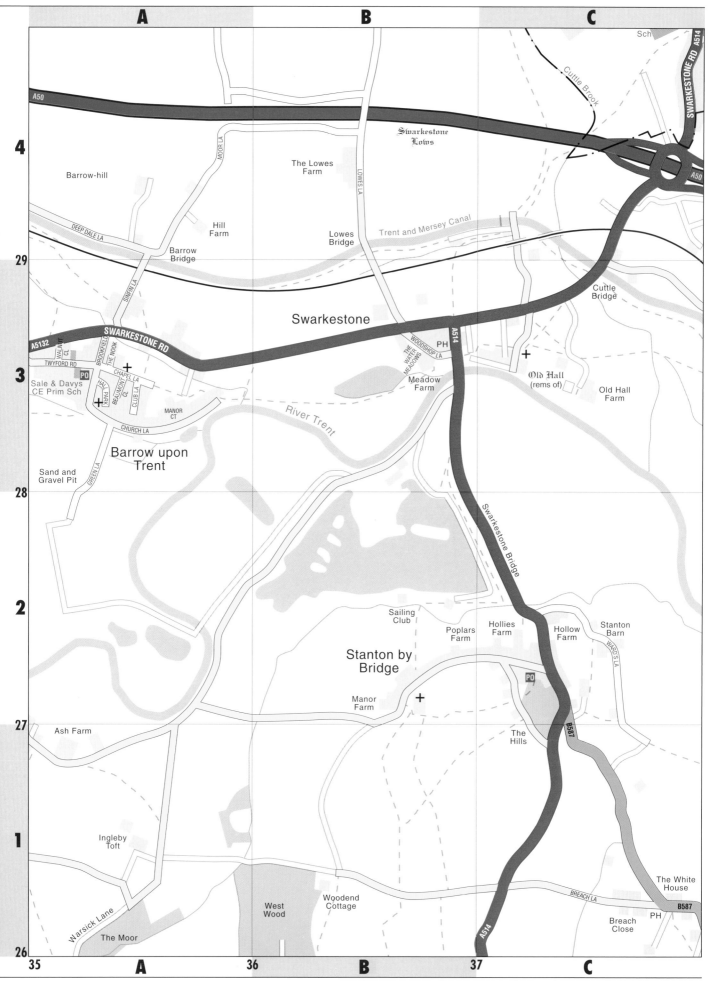

4

Barrow-hill

The Lowes
Farm

Swarkestone
Lows

Sch

A514

SWARKESTONE RD

Cuttle Brook

A50

MOOR LA

Hill
Farm

DEEP DALE LA

Barrow
Bridge

29

Lowes
Bridge

LOWES LA

Trent and Mersey Canal

Cuttle
Bridge

SINFIN LA

Swarkestone

A5132

SWARKESTONE RD

WALNUT CL

BROOKFIELD

THE NOOK

TWYFORD RD

PO

CHAPEL LA

THE WATER MEADOWS

THE WOODSHOP LA

PH

A514

Old Hall
(rems of)

Old Hall
Farm

3

Sale & Davys
CE Prim Sch

HALL PARK

BEAUMONT CL

CLUB LA

MANOR
CT

Meadow
Farm

Barrow upon
Trent

CHURCH LA

River Trent

GREEN LA

Sand and
Gravel Pit

28

Swarkestone Bridge

2

Sailing
Club

Poplars
Farm

Hollies
Farm

Hollow
Farm

Stanton
Barn

WARD'S LA

Stanton by
Bridge

PO

Manor
Farm

27

Ash Farm

The
Hills

B587

Ingleby
Toft

1

BREACH LA

The White
House

B587

Warsick Lane

The Moor

West
Wood

Woodend
Cottage

A514

Breach
Close

PH

26

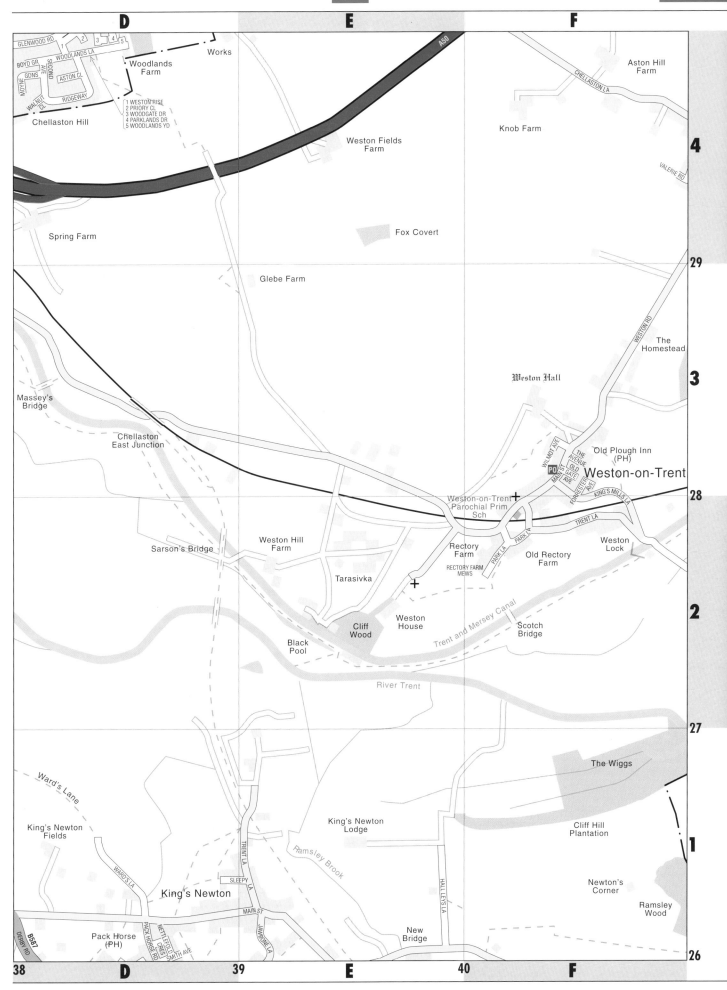

D **E** **F**

GLENWOOD RD

BOYD GR
AVE
GDNS
MONUM
SECOND AVE
ASTON CL
WOODLANDS LA
Works

Woodlands
Farm

WALNUT
CL
RIDGEWAY

Chellaston Hill

1 WESTON RISE
2 PRIORY CL
3 WOODGATE DR
4 PARKLANDS DR
5 WOODLANDS YD

A50

Weston Fields
Farm

Knob Farm

Aston Hill
Farm

CHELLASTON LA

VALERIE RD

4

Spring Farm

Fox Covert

29

Glebe Farm

WESTON RD

The
Homestead

Massey's
Bridge

Weston Hall

3

Chellaston
East Junction

Old Plough Inn
(PH)

WILMOT AVE

THE
AVENUE
OLD
GATE

MAIN ST

PO

FORRESTER AVE
KING'S MILLS LA

Weston-on-Trent

28

Weston-on-Trent
Parochial Prim
Sch

Sarson's Bridge

Weston Hill
Farm

Rectory
Farm

PARK LA

PARK LA

Old Rectory
Farm

TRENT LA

Weston
Lock

Tarasivka

RECTORY FARM
MEWS

Weston
House

Cliff
Wood

Trent and Mersey Canal

Scotch
Bridge

2

Black
Pool

River Trent

27

The Wiggs

Ward's Lane

King's Newton
Fields

King's Newton
Lodge

Cliff Hill
Plantation

WARD'S LA

TRENT LA

Ramsley Brook

HALL LEYS LA

1

Newton's
Corner

SLEEPY
LA

King's Newton

Ramsley
Wood

B587
DERBY RD

Pack Horse
(PH)

PACK HORSE RD
NETTLEFOLD
CRES
SMITH AVE

MAIN ST

JAWBONE LA

New
Bridge

26

38 **D** **39** **E** **40** **F**

Index

Street names are listed alphabetically and show the locality, the Postcode District, the page number and a reference to the square in which the name falls on the map page

Edgelaw Ct 10 Derby DE24........ **15** E2

Full street name
This may have been abbreviated on the map

Location Number
If present, this indicates the street's position on a congested area of the map instead of the name

Town, village or locality in which the street falls.

Postcode District for the street name

Page number of the map on which the street name appears

Grid square in which the centre of the street falls

Schools, hospitals, sports centres, railway stations, shopping centres, industrial estates, public amenities and other places of interest are also listed.

Abbreviations used in the index

App	Approach	Cl	Close	Ent	Enterprise	La	Lane	Rdbt	Roundabout
Arc	Arcade	Comm	Common	Espl	Esplanade	N	North	S	South
Ave	Avenue	Cnr	Corner	Est	Estate	Orch	Orchard	Sq	Square
Bvd	Boulevard	Cotts	Cottages	Gdns	Gardens	Par	Parade	Strs	Stairs
Bldgs	Buildings	Ct	Court	Gn	Green	Pk	Park	Stps	Steps
Bsns Pk	Business Park	Ctyd	Courtyard	Gr	Grove	Pas	Passage	St	Street, Saint
Bsns Ctr	Business Centre	Cres	Crescent	Hts	Heights	Pl	Place	Terr	Terrace
Bglws	Bungalows	Dr	Drive	Ho	House	Prec	Precinct	Trad Est	Trading Estate
Cswy	Causeway	Dro	Drove	Ind Est	Industrial Estate	Prom	Promenade	Wlk	Walk
Ctr	Centre	E	East	Intc	Interchange	Ret Pk	Retail Park	W	West
Cir	Circus	Emb	Embankment	Junc	Junction	Rd	Road	Yd	Yard

Abbey Hill
Breadsall DE21, DE22 ... 7 D2
Derby DE21, DE22 ... 7 D2
Abbey Hill Rd DE22 ... 6 B1
Abbey La DE22 ... 7 D1
Abbey Yd DE22 ... 7 D1
Abbeyfields Cl DE22 ... 7 D1
Abbot Cl DE21 ... 7 F1
Abbots Gr DE56 ... 3 D3
Aberdare Cl DE21 ... 8 A1
Abingdon Bsns Ctr The DE24 ... 11 E1
Abingdon St DE24 ... 16 B4
Abney Cl DE3 ... 9 F1
Acacia Ave DE3 ... 9 F1
Acer Croft DE21 ... 7 F2
Acorn Cl DE24 ... 16 C2
Acorn Dr DE56 ... 3 D3
Acorn Way Belper DE56 ... 3 D3
Derby DE21 ... 12 B3
Morley DE21 ... 12 B3
Acrefield Way DE73 ... 17 D1
Acton Rd DE22 ... 9 F3
Adam's Rd DE6 ... 9 D4
Addison Rd DE24 ... 16 B4
Adelaide Cl DE3 ... 9 F2
Adelphi Cl DE23 ... 15 D3
Adrian St DE24 ... 16 B3
Adwick Cl DE3 ... 9 E1
Agard St DE1 ... 10 C3
Ainley Cl DE24 ... 16 C4
Ainsworth Dr DE23 ... 15 F4
Airedale Wlk DE24 ... 17 E3
Albany Rd DE22 ... 10 B2
Albemarle Rd DE21 ... 12 A4
Albert Cres DE21 ... 12 A2
Albert Rd DE21 ... 12 A2
Albert St DE56 ... 2 C2
Albrighton Ave DE24 ... 15 E1
Alder Cl DE21 ... 7 F2
Alder Ct DE1 ... 11 D4
Alder Rd DE56 ... 3 D2
Alderfen Cl DE24 ... 16 B2
Alderley Ct DE21 ... 8 A1
Aldersgate DE22 ... 9 F4
Aldersley Cl DE65 ... 14 B1
Aldwych DE22 ... 10 A3
Alexandra Gdns DE23 ... 11 E1
Alexandre Cl DE23 ... 15 E3
Alfreton Rd Breadsall DE21 ... 7 E3
Derby DE21 ... 7 E3
Holbrook DE21 ... 5 E1
Little Eaton DE21 ... 7 E3
Alison Cl DE21 ... 11 F4
All Saints Ct DE3 ... 9 E1
Allan Ave DE23 ... 14 C4
Allen St DE24 ... 16 C3
Allenpark Inf Sch DE24 ... 16 B3
Allenton Com Prim Sch DE24 ... 16 B3
Allestree Cl DE24 ... 16 C4
Allestree La DE22 ... 6 B2
Allestree St DE24 ... 16 C4
Allstone Lee DE56 ... 2 C3
Alma Hts DE3 ... 9 F1
Alport Cl DE56 ... 3 D3
Alsager Cl DE21 ... 8 A1
Alstonfield Dr DE22 ... 6 C1
Alton Cl DE22 ... 6 B2
Alton Rd DE56 ... 3 E2
Alum Cl DE24 ... 17 E4
Alvaston Inf Sch DE24 ... 17 E3
Alvaston Jun Com Sch DE24 ... 17 E4
Alvaston St DE24 ... 17 D4
Alverton Cl DE3 ... 9 E1
Alward's Cl DE24 ... 17 D3
Amber Ct DE56 ... 3 D3
Amber Rd DE22 ... 6 B1
Amber St DE24 ... 16 B4
Amberley Dr DE24 ... 15 F3
Ambrose Terr DE1 ... 10 C3
Amesbury La DE21 ... 7 F1
Amy St DE22 ... 10 C2
Anderson St DE24 ... 16 C4
Andrew Cl DE23 ... 14 C4
Anglers' La DE21 ... 12 C2
Anglesey St DE21 ... 11 E4
Anne Potter Cl DE72 ... 13 E3
Anstey Ct DE21 ... 8 A1
Anthony Cres DE24 ... 16 C3
Anthony Dr DE24 ... 16 C3
Appian Cl DE72 ... 13 E1
Appian Way DE24 ... 17 E3
Appleby Ct DE22 ... 10 C2
Appledore Dr DE21 ... 8 A1
Applegate Cl DE21 ... 8 A2
Appleton Cl DE21 ... 12 A4
Appleton Dr DE56 ... 3 D3
Appletree Cl DE72 ... 13 E1
Applewood Cl DE56 ... 3 D3
Arboretum Prim Sch DE23 ... 11 D1
Archer St DE24 ... 11 F1
Arden Cl DE23 ... 10 C1
Ardleigh Cl DE3 ... 14 B4
Argyle St DE22 ... 10 C2
Argyll Cl DE21 ... 12 C3
Arkendale Wlk DE24 ... 17 E3
Arkwright Ave DE56 ... 3 E3
Arkwright St DE24 ... 16 B4
Arleston La DE24 ... 15 E1
Arleston St DE23 ... 15 F4
Arlington Dr DE24 ... 16 C3
Arlington Rd DE23 ... 10 B1
Armscote Cl DE21 ... 8 A1
Arnhem Terr DE21 ... 12 C2
Arnold St DE22 ... 10 B3
Arran Cl DE24 ... 15 F2
Arridge Rd DE21 ... 11 F3
Arthur Ct DE23 ... 11 D1
Arthur Hind Cl DE22 ... 10 C4
Arundel Ave DE3 ... 9 F1
Arundel Dr DE21 ... 12 C3
Arundel St DE22 ... 10 B2
Ascot Dr DE24 ... 16 B4
Ash Acre DE56 ... 3 E2
Ash Cl DE22 ... 6 B2
Ash Croft Prim Sch DE24 ... 15 F1
Ash Tree Cl
Breadsall DE21 ... 7 F2
Duffield DE56 ... 4 C3
Ashbourne Ct DE22 ... 10 C3
Ashbourne Rd Belper DE56 ... 2 B2
Derby DE22 ... 10 B4
Mackworth DE22 ... 9 F4
Shottle DE56 ... 1 E2
Turnditch DE56 ... 1 E2
Ashbrook Ave DE72 ... 13 E1
Ashbrook Cl DE22 ... 6 B2
Ashbrook Inf & Jun Sch DE72 ... 13 D1
Ashby St DE24 ... 16 C3
Ashcombe Gdns DE21 ... 8 A1
Ashcroft Cl DE24 ... 16 C4
Ashe Pl DE23 ... 10 C1
Ashfield Ave DE21 ... 11 F4
Ashford Rise DE56 ... 3 E3
Ashgate Inf & Jun Sch DE22 ... 10 B3
Ashgrove Ct DE21 ... 8 A1
Ashleigh Dr DE73 ... 16 C1
Ashley St DE22 ... 10 B3
Ashmeadow DE72 ... 13 D1
Ashop Rd DE56 ... 3 E3
Ashopton Ave DE23 ... 15 F4
Ashover Cl DE21 ... 11 F4
Ashover Rd
Derby, Allestree DE22 ... 6 B1
Derby, Chaddesden DE21 ... 11 F4
Ashton Cl DE3 ... 9 E2
Ashton Way DE56 ... 3 E2
Ashtree Ave DE24 ... 16 A3
Ashwater Cl DE24 ... 15 F1
Ashworth Ave DE21 ... 11 F3
Askerfield Ave DE22 ... 6 B2
Aspen Dr DE21 ... 12 B2
Asterdale Prim Sch DE21 ... 12 C2
Asterdale View DE21 ... 12 C2
Astlow Dr DE56 ... 3 D3
Aston Cl DE73 ... 19 D4
Aston La DE73 ... 17 D1
Aston Rd DE23 ... 15 E3
Astorville Park Rd DE73 ... 16 C1
Atchison Gdns DE21 ... 12 A4
Athlone Cl DE21 ... 11 E4
Athol Cl DE24 ... 15 F2
Atlow Rd DE21 ... 11 F4
Attlebridge Cl DE21 ... 11 E4
Atworth Gr DE23 ... 14 C3
Auckland Cl DE3 ... 9 F2
Audrey Dr DE21 ... 12 A4
Augusta St DE23 ... 11 D1
Aults Cl DE65 ... 14 B1
Austen Ave DE23 ... 15 D4
Austin Sq DE23 ... 15 F4
Autumn Gr DE21 ... 11 F3
Avenue Rd DE56 ... 4 C3
Avenue The Belper DE56 ... 2 C1
Derby, Chaddesden DE21 ... 11 F3
Weston-on-T DE72 ... 19 F3
Averham Cl DE21 ... 8 A1
Aviemore Way DE24 ... 15 F2
Avocet Ct 2 DE24 ... 15 E2
Avon Cl DE24 ... 15 E1
Avon St DE24 ... 16 C4
Avondale Rd DE21 ... 12 B3
Avonmouth Dr DE24 ... 16 C4
Aycliffe Gdns DE24 ... 16 C2
Aylesbury Ave DE21 ... 11 F4
Ayr Cl DE21 ... 12 B2

Babbacombe Cl DE24 ... 17 E4
Babington Hospl DE56 ... 2 C1
Back La DE73 ... 17 D1
Back Wyver La DE56 ... 2 C3
Backhouse La DE72 ... 13 E3
Badger Cl DE21 ... 12 C3
Bagshaw St DE24 ... 16 C4
Bainbridge St DE23 ... 11 D2
Bains Dr DE72 ... 13 E1
Bakeacre La DE65 ... 14 C2
Baker St DE24 ... 16 C4
Bakewell Cl DE3 ... 9 F2
Bakewell St DE22 ... 10 C2
Balaclava Rd DE23 ... 16 A4
Balfour Rd DE23 ... 16 A4
Balham Wlk DE22 ... 10 A3
Ballards Way DE72 ... 13 E1
Ballater Cl DE24 ... 15 F2
Balleny Cl DE21 ... 7 F1
Balmoral Cl DE23 ... 10 A1
Balmoral Rd DE72 ... 13 E1
Bamburgh Cl DE21 ... 12 B2
Bamford Ave DE23 ... 15 F4
Bancroft Dr DE22 ... 6 B2
Bangor St DE21 ... 11 F4
Bank Side DE22 ... 6 C1
Bank View Rd DE22 ... 10 C4
Bankfield Dr DE21 ... 12 C2
Bankholmes Cl DE24 ... 15 F1
Bannels Ave DE23 ... 15 D4
Banwell Cl DE3 ... 9 E2
Barchester Cl DE21 ... 8 A1
Barden Dr DE22 ... 6 C2
Bardsey Ct DE21 ... 8 A2
Bare La DE72 ... 13 E3
Barf Cl DE3 ... 9 F1
Bargate Cl DE56 ... 3 E1
Bargate Rd DE56 ... 3 D1
Barley Cft DE73 ... 16 C1
Barley Cl DE21 ... 7 E4
Barley Croft DE56 ... 3 D1
Barleycorn Cl DE21 ... 8 B1
Barn Cl Findern DE65 ... 14 B1
Quarndon DE22 ... 6 B3
Barnard Rd DE21 ... 7 E1
Barnes Gn DE22 ... 10 A4
Barnhill Gr DE23 ... 15 D4
Barnstaple Cl DE21 ... 8 A1
Barnwood Cl DE3 ... 9 E1
Baron Cl DE21 ... 8 B2
Barrett St DE24 ... 17 D4
Barrie Dr DE24 ... 15 F3
Barron's Way DE72 ... 13 E1
Barrow La DE73 ... 18 B3
Barton Cl DE21 ... 12 C3
Barton Knoll DE56 ... 3 E2
Barton Knowle DE56 ... 3 E2
Basildon Cl DE24 ... 16 C3
Baslow Dr DE22 ... 6 C2
Bass St DE22 ... 10 B3
Bassingham Cl DE21 ... 8 A1
Bateman St DE23 ... 11 E2
Bath Rd DE3 ... 9 F1
Baverstock Cl DE73 ... 16 C2
Baxter Sq DE23 ... 15 F3
Bayleaf Cres DE21 ... 8 A2
Bayswater Cl DE22 ... 9 F3
Beardmore Cl DE21 ... 7 F1
Beatty St DE24 ... 16 C4
Beaufort Ct Ind Est DE21 ... 11 E4
Beaufort Inf & Jun Schs DE21 ... 11 E4
Beaufort Rd DE24 ... 15 E1
Beaufort St DE21 ... 11 E4
Beaumaris Ct DE21 ... 12 C3
Beaumont Cl
Barrow u T DE73 ... 18 A3
Belper DE56 ... 3 E2
Beaumont Wlk DE23 ... 15 F3
Beaurepaire Cres DE56 ... 3 D3
Beaureper Ave DE22 ... 6 C2
Becher St DE23 ... 11 D1
Beckenham Way DE22 ... 10 A3
Becket Prim Sch DE22 ... 10 C2
Beckitt Cl DE24 ... 17 D4
Becksitch La DE56 ... 2 C1
Bedford Cl DE22 ... 10 B2
Bedford St DE22 ... 10 B2
Beech Ave Borrowash DE72 ... 13 E2
Derby DE24 ... 17 D4
Quarndon DE22 ... 6 A4
Beech Cl DE56 ... 3 D2
Beech Ct DE21 ... 12 B3
Beech Dr Derby DE22 ... 10 C4
Findern DE65 ... 14 C1
Beech Gdns DE24 ... 17 D4
Beech Wlk DE23 ... 10 B1
Beechcroft DE21 ... 7 E2
Beeches Ave DE21 ... 12 B3
Beechley Dr DE21 ... 8 A1
Beechwood Cl DE56 ... 2 C3
Beechwood Cres DE23 ... 15 E4
Beeley Cl Belper DE56 ... 3 E3
Derby, Allestree DE22 ... 6 B1
Derby, Oakwood DE22 ... 7 F1
Belfast Wlk DE21 ... 12 A2
Belfry Cl DE3 ... 9 F1
Belgrave Cl DE56 ... 3 E3
Belle Acre Cl DE56 ... 2 C2
Bellingham Ct DE22 ... 6 B1
Belmont Dr DE72 ... 13 D1
Belper La DE56 ... 2 C3

Belper Rd Derby DE1 10 C4
Holbrook DE56 5 E4
Kilburn DE56 3 F1
Belper Sch DE56 3 E2
Belper Sports Ctr DE56 3 E2
Belper Sta DE56 2 C2
Belsize Cl DE22 9 F3
Belvedere Cl DE3 9 E2
Belvoir St DE23 10 C1
Bembridge Dr DE24 17 E3
Bemrose Com Sch DE22 10 B2
Bemrose Mews DE22 10 B2
Bemrose Rd DE24 16 C4
Bendall Gn DE23 15 E3
Benmore Ct DE21 8 A2
Bennett St DE24 16 B3
Bensley Cl DE73 17 D1
Benson St DE24 16 C4
Bentley St DE24 16 C3
Beresford Dr DE21 12 C2
Berkeley Cl DE23 15 E4
Berkshire St DE21 11 E4
Bermuda Ave DE21 7 E3
Berry Park Cl DE22 6 C1
Berwick Ave DE21 11 E4
Berwick Cl DE24 17 D3
Berwick Dr DE24 15 E2
Bessalone Dr DE56 3 D3
Besthorpe Cl DE21 8 A1
Bethulie Rd DE23 16 A4
Betjeman Sq DE24 16 A3
Beverley St DE24 11 E1
Bewdley Cl DE73 17 D2
Bicester Ave DE24 15 E1
Bickley Moss DE21 8 A1
Bideford Dr DE23 15 E3
Bingham St DE24 16 C3
Binscombe La DE21 7 F2
Birch View Ct DE1 10 C4
Birches Rd DE22 6 B2
Birchfield Cl DE73 16 C1
Birchover Rise DE21 7 F1
Birchover Way DE22 6 C1
Birchview Cl DE56 3 D1
Birchwood Ave DE23 15 E3
Birdcage Wlk DE22 9 F3
Birdwood St DE23 10 C1
Birkdale Cl DE3 10 A1
Biscay Ct DE21 8 B1
Bishop Lonsdale CE Prim Sch DE22 10 C2
Bishop's Dr DE21 7 F1
Blaby Cl DE23 15 F3
Blackberry Way DE56 3 F1
Blackbird Row DE56 3 E1
Blackden Cl DE56 3 F2
Blackmore St DE23 15 F4
Blackmount Ct 7 DE24 15 E2
Blackthorn Cl DE73 7 F1
Blackthorne Cl DE56 3 F1
Blagreaves Ave DE23 15 E3
Blagreaves La DE23 15 E3
Blakebrook Dr DE73 17 D2
Blakeney Ct DE21 8 B1
Blandford Cl DE24 17 E3
Blankney Cl DE24 15 E1
Blencathra Dr DE3 14 C4
Blenheim Dr DE22 6 B2
Blithfield Gdns DE73 17 D1
Bluebell Cl DE24 15 E1
Bluebird Ct DE24 15 E2
Blyth Pl DE21 7 E1
Boden St DE23 11 D1
Bodmin Cl DE24 15 E2
Boman's La DE56 1 F4
Bonchurch Cl DE24 17 E3
Bonnyrigg Dr DE21 8 A1
Bonsall Dr DE3 9 F2
Booth St DE24 16 C4
Boothgate DE56 3 F4
Border Cres DE24 17 D3
Borrow Wood Inf & Jun Schs DE21 12 C3
Borrowash By-pass
Borrowash DE72 13 E2
Derby DE21 12 B2
Risley DE72 13 E2
Borrowash Rd DE21 12 C2
Borrowfield Rd DE21 12 C2
Borrowfields DE72 13 D1
Boscastle Rd DE24 17 D3
Bosley Mews DE56 2 C3
Bosnall Ave DE23 15 E4
Boston Cl DE21 12 B3
Boswell Sq DE23 15 F4
Bosworth Ave DE23 15 F3
Boulton Dr DE24 17 D3
Boulton Inf Sch DE24 17 D3
Boulton Jun Sch DE24 17 D3
Boulton La
Derby, Allenton DE24 16 C3
Derby, Boulton DE24 17 D3
Boundary Rd DE22 10 C2
Bowbridge Ave DE23 15 E3
Bower St DE24 16 C4
Bowland Cl DE3 9 F1
Bowlees Ct DE23 14 C4
Bowmer Rd DE24 11 F1
Boxmoor Cl DE23 14 C4
Boyd Gr DE73 19 D4
Boylestone Rd DE23 15 E3
Bracken's La DE24 16 C3
Brackens Ave DE24 16 C3
Brackensdale Ave DE22 10 A3
Brackensdale Inf Sch DE22 10 A3
Brackensdale Jun Sch DE22 10 A3
Brackley DE56 3 F1
Brackley Dr DE21 12 C3
Bracknell Dr DE24 16 C3
Bradbourne Ct DE22 10 C2
Bradbury Cl DE72 13 E1
Bradgate Ct DE23 15 F3
Brading Cl DE24 17 E3
Bradley Dr DE56 3 D2
Bradley St DE22 10 C4
Bradmoor Gr DE73 17 D1
Bradshaw Croft DE56 2 C3
Bradshaw Dr DE56 5 E3
Bradwell Cl DE3 9 F1
Bradwell Way DE56 3 D3
Braemar Cl 12 DE24 15 E2
Brafield Cl DE56 3 E2
Brailsford Rd DE21 11 F4
Braintree Cl DE21 7 E1
Braithwell Cl DE22 6 C1
Bramble Mews DE3 9 E1
Bramble Way DE56 3 F1
Brambleberry Ct DE21 8 A2
Bramfield Ave DE22 10 C2
Bramfield Ct DE22 10 C2
Bramley Cl DE21 8 B2
Brampton Cl DE3 9 E2
Brampton Ct DE56 3 E2
Brandelhow Ct DE21 8 B2
Branksome Ave DE24 17 E4
Brassington Rd DE21 7 D4
Brayfield Ave DE23 15 E4
Brayfield Rd DE23 15 E4
Breach La DE73 18 C1
Breadsall CE Prim Sch DE21 7 F2
Breadsall Hill Top Inf & Jun Sch DE21 7 F1
Brecon Cl DE21 12 C3
Breedon Ave DE23 15 E3
Breedon Hill Rd DE23 10 C2
Brentford Dr DE22 10 A3
Bretby Sq DE23 15 E3
Bretton Ave DE23 10 B1
Bretton Rd DE56 3 F3
Breydon Cl DE24 16 B2
Briar Cl Borrowash DE72 13 E1
Derby DE21 12 A2
Briar Lea Cl DE24 15 F2
Briarsgate DE22 6 B1
Briarwood Way DE23 15 E3
Brick Row DE22 7 D1
Brick St DE1 10 C3
Brickkiln La DE7 8 B4
Brickyard La DE56 3 F1
Bridge Foot DE56 2 C3
Bridge Hill DE56 2 C3
Bridge St Belper DE56 2 C2
Derby DE1 10 C3
Bridge View DE56 5 D4
Bridgend Ct DE21 8 B1
Bridgeness Rd DE23 14 C3
Bridgeport Rd DE21 12 B3
Bridgwater Cl DE24 17 E4
Bridle Cl DE73 17 D1
Brierfield Way DE3 14 C4
Brigden Ave DE24 16 C4
Brighstone Cl DE24 17 E3
Bright St DE22 10 B3
Brighton Rd DE24 16 C4
Brigmor Wlk DE22 10 B3
Brindley Wlk DE24 15 F1
Brisbane Rd DE3 9 F2
Briset Cl DE24 15 F1
Bristol Dr DE3 9 F1
Broad Bank DE22 10 C4
Broad La DE72 17 F2
Broadfields Cl DE22 10 C4
Broadholme La DE56 3 D4
Broadleaf Cl DE21 7 F1
Broadway Derby DE22 10 C4
Duffield DE56 4 C1
Broadway Park Cl DE22 10 C4
Brockley DE21 12 C3
Bromley St DE22 10 C4
Brompton Rd DE22 9 F3
Bromyard Dr DE73 17 D2
Bronte Pl DE23 15 D4
Brook Cl Findern DE65 14 B1
Quarndon DE22 6 B2
Brook Rd Borrowash DE72 13 E1
Elvaston DE72 17 F2
Brookfield DE73 18 A3
Brookfield Ave
Derby, Chaddesden DE21 12 A4
Derby, Littleover DE23 15 E3
Brookfield Prim Sch DE3 14 B4
Brookfields DE56 5 F4
Brookfields Dr DE21 7 E2
Brookhouse St DE24 16 B3
Brooklands Dr DE23 15 E4
Brooks Hollow DE21 7 E4
Brookside DE56 2 C2
Brookside Cl DE1 10 C4
Brookside Rd DE21 7 F2
Brookside Specl Sch DE21 7 F2
Broom Cl Belper DE56 2 C3
Derby, Chellaston DE73 16 C1
Derby, Sinfin DE73 15 F1
Duffield DE56 4 B2
Broomfield Coll (Derbyshire Coll of Ag) DE7 8 A3
Broomhill Cl DE3 9 E2
Brough St DE22 10 B3
Broughton Ave DE23 10 B1
Brown's La DE56 5 E4
Browning Cir DE23 15 F4
Browning St DE23 15 F4
Brun La Kirk Langley DE6 9 D4
Mackworth DE22 9 D4
Brunswick St DE23 15 F4
Brunswood Cl DE21 12 C3
Brunton Cl DE3 9 E1
Bryony Cl DE21 8 A1
Buchan St DE24 16 B4
Buckingham Ave DE21 11 E4
Buckland Cl DE1 10 C3
Buckminster Cl DE21 7 F1
Buller St DE23 10 C1
Bullpit La DE56 7 D4
Bullsmoor DE56 3 E2
Buntings Cl DE3 10 A2
Burbage Cl DE56 3 E3
Burbage Pl DE24 16 C4
Burdock Cl DE21 7 F1
Burghley Cl DE73 16 C1
Burghley Way DE23 14 C3
Burleigh Dr DE22 10 C4
Burley Dr DE22 6 C4
Burley Hill DE22, DE56 7 D4
Burley La DE22 6 C4
Burlington Rd DE22 9 F3
Burlington Way DE3 9 E1
Burnaby St DE24 16 C4
Burnage Ct DE22 10 C2
Burnham Dr DE3 9 E1
Burns Cl DE23 15 D4
Burnside Cl DE24 15 E2
Burnside Dr DE21 12 C2
Burnside St DE24 17 D4
Burrowfield Mews DE21 12 C1
Burton Rd Derby DE23 10 B1
Findern DE65 14 B2
Bush Vale DE56 2 C3
Buttermere Dr DE22 6 C2
Buttonoak Dr DE73 17 D2
Butts The DE56 3 D2
Buxton Dr Derby DE3 9 F2
Little Eaton DE21 5 E1
Buxton Rd DE21 11 F4
Byfield Cl DE21 8 A1
Byng Ave DE23 15 F4
Byron St DE23 10 C1
Bywell La DE56 3 F1

Cadgwith Dr DE22 6 C2
Cadwell Cl DE24 17 E3
Caerhays Ct DE24 15 E2
Caernarvon Cl DE21 12 C3
Caesar St DE1 11 D4
Cairngorm Dr DE24 15 E2
Cairns Cl DE3 9 F2
Calder Cl DE22 6 C2
Caldermill Dr DE21 8 A1
California Gdns DE22 10 B2
Calladine La DE56 1 E3
Callow Hill Way DE23 15 D4
Calver Cl Belper DE56 3 D3
Derby DE21 7 F2
Calverton Cl DE24 16 C2
Calvin Cl DE24 17 D3
Camberwell Ave DE22 10 A3
Camborne Cl DE21 7 F1
Cambridge St
Derby, Rose Hill DE23 11 D1
Derby, Spondon DE21 12 C2
Camden St DE22 10 B2
Camellia Cl DE3 9 E2
Cameron Rd DE23 15 F4
Camp St DE1 11 D4
Camp Wood Cl DE21 7 E4
Campbell St Belper DE56 2 C2
Derby DE24 16 B4
Campion St DE22 10 B3
Campsie Ct 6 DE24 15 E2
Canada St DE56 3 D1
Canberra Cl DE3 9 F1
Canon's Wlk DE22 6 C1
Canterbury Cl DE56 4 C2
Canterbury St DE21 11 F4
Cantley Cl DE24 16 B2
Cardales Cl DE65 14 B1
Cardean Cl DE1 11 D4
Cardigan St DE21 11 E4
Cardrona Cl DE21 7 F1
Carisbrooke Gdns DE23 15 E3
Carlisle Ave DE23 15 D4
Carlton Ave DE24 16 C2
Carlton Dr DE24 16 C2
Carlton Gdns DE24 16 C2
Carlton Rd DE23 10 C1
Carlyle Inf Sch DE23 15 D4
Carlyle St DE24 15 F3
Carnegie St DE23 16 A4
Carnforth Cl DE3 9 F1
Carnoustie Cl DE3 9 F1
Carol Cres DE21 11 F3
Caroline Cl DE24 17 E4
Carron Cl DE24 15 F2
Carsington Cres DE22 6 B1
Carsington Mews DE22 6 C1
Carson Rd DE21 12 A3
Carter St DE24 16 B3
Cascade Gr DE23 15 D4
Casson Ave DE24 17 D3
Castings Rd DE23 16 A4
Castle Croft DE24 17 E3
Castle Ct DE21 17 F3
Castle Hill Duffield DE56 4 C2
Findern DE65 14 B1
Castle Orch DE56 4 C2
Castlecraig Ct DE24 15 F1
Castleshaw Dr DE23 14 C4
Castleton Ave DE23 15 F4
Cathedral View DE22 10 B1
Catherine St DE23 11 D1
Catterick Dr DE3 9 E1
Causeway DE22 6 C1
Cavan Dr DE21 12 A2
Cavendish Ave DE22 6 C2
Cavendish Cl DE56 4 B1
Cavendish Close Inf & Jun Schs DE21 12 A4
Cavendish Way DE3 9 F1
Caversfield Cl DE23 15 D4
Caxton St
Derby, Littleover DE23 15 F3
Derby, Normanton DE23 15 F4
Cecil St DE22 10 B3
Cedar Dr DE72 13 E2
Cedar Gr DE56 3 D1
Cedar St DE22 10 C4
Cedarwood Ct DE21 7 F1
Celandine Cl DE21 8 A1
Celanese Rd DE21 12 B2
Cemetery Rd DE56 3 D3
Central Ave DE72 13 D1
Centurion Wlk DE1 11 D4
Chaddesden La DE21 12 A3
Chaddesden Lane End DE21 11 F3
Chaddesden Park Inf & Jun Schs DE21 12 A4
Chaddesden Park Rd DE21 11 F4
Chadfield Rd DE56 4 C3
Chadwick Ave DE24 16 C3
Chaffinch Cl DE21 12 C3
Chain La DE3 10 A1
Chalfont Sq DE21 8 A1
Chalkley Cl DE24 16 C4
Challis Ave DE21 12 A4
Chambers St DE24 11 F1
Champion Hill DE56 4 C2
Chancery La DE22 10 A3
Chandlers Ford DE21 7 F1
Chandos Pole St DE22 10 B3
Chandres Ct DE22 6 C2
Chantry Cl DE73 9 E1
Chapel La Barrow u T DE73 18 A3
Derby, Chaddesden DE21 12 A4
Derby, Chellaston DE73 17 D1
Derby, Spondon DE21 12 C3
Chapel Row DE72 13 D1
Chapel Side DE21 12 C3
Chapel St Belper DE56 2 C2
Derby, Spondon DE21 12 C3
Duffield DE56 4 C2
Holbrook DE56 5 E4
Chapman Ave DE24 17 D3
Chapter Cl DE21 7 E1
Charingworth Rd DE21 8 A1
Chariot Cl DE24 17 E3
Charlbury Cl DE23 15 D4
Charles Ave DE21 12 B3
Charleston Rd DE21 12 B3
Charlestown Dr DE22 6 B2
Charlotte St DE23 11 D1
Charnwood Ave
Belper DE56 3 D2
Borrowash DE72 13 E1
Derby DE23 15 E3
Charterhouse Cl DE21 7 F2
Charterstone La DE22 6 C2
Chartwell Dr DE21 11 E3
Chase The Derby DE24 15 F2
Little Eaton DE21 5 E1
Chatham Ct DE56 3 E2
Chatham St DE23 16 A4
Chatsworth Cres DE22 6 C2
Chatsworth Ct DE24 15 F2
Chatsworth Dr Derby DE3 9 F2
Little Eaton DE21 5 E1
Chatsworth St DE23 10 C1
Chatteris Dr DE21 7 E1
Cheadle Cl DE23 10 A1
Cheam Cl DE22 9 F3
Cheapside DE56 2 C2
Chedworth Dr DE24 17 E3
Chellaston Inf Sch DE73 17 D1
Chellaston Jun Sch DE73 16 C1
Chellaston La DE73 17 E1
Chellaston Park Ct DE73 16 C1
Chellaston Rd DE24 16 C2
Chellaston Sch DE73 16 C1
Chelmarsh Cl DE73 17 D2
Chelmorton Pl DE21 11 F4
Chelmsford Cl DE3 9 E2
Chelsea Cl DE22 9 F3
Chelwood Rd DE73 16 C1
Chequer La DE56 1 F4
Chequers La DE21 11 E3
Chequers Rd DE21 11 E3
Cheriton Gdns DE23 14 C4
Cherry Tree Ave DE56 3 D3
Cherry Tree Hill Inf & Jun Schs DE21 12 A3
Cherry Tree Mews DE21 12 A2
Cherrybrook Dr DE21 8 A2
Chertsey Rd DE3 9 E1
Chesapeake Rd DE21 12 A3
Cheshire St DE24 16 C3
Chester Ave DE22 7 D3
Chester Ct DE21 12 C2
Chester Green Rd DE1 11 D4
Chesterfield Rd DE56 3 D2
Chesterford Ct DE23 14 C3
Chesterton Ave DE23 15 F4
Chesterton Rd DE21 12 C3
Chestnut Ave Belper DE56 3 D1
Derby, Chellaston DE73 16 C2
Derby, Mickleover DE73 9 E2
Derby, Rose Hill DE23 11 D1
Holbrook DE56 5 E4
Chestnut Cl DE56 4 C1
Chestnut Gr DE72 13 E2
Chevely Ct DE21 11 E4
Cheverton Cl DE24 17 E3
Chevin Ave
Borrowash DE72 13 E1
Derby DE72 9 F1
Chevin Bank DE56 4 B3
Chevin Pl DE1 10 C4
Chevin Rd
Belper, Chevinside DE56 2 C1
Belper, Milford DE56 4 C4
Derby DE1 10 C4
Duffield DE56 4 C3
Chevin Vale DE56 4 C3
Chevin View DE56 2 C2
Cheviot St DE22 10 B3
Cheyenne Gdns DE21 12 B3
Cheyne Wlk DE22 10 B3
Chilson Dr DE3 9 E2
Chime Cl DE21 7 F1
Chingford Ct DE22 10 A3
Chinley Rd DE21 8 A1
Chiswick Cl DE22 9 F3
Church Cl DE73 17 D1
Church Hill DE21 12 B2
Church La Barrow u T DE73 18 A3
Belper DE56 3 D2
Breadsall DE21 7 F2
Derby, Chaddesden DE21 12 A3
Derby, Darley Abbey DE22 7 D1
Little Eaton DE21 7 E4
Mackworth DE22 9 F4
Morley DE7 8 C3
Church La N DE22 6 C2
Church Mews DE21 12 B2
Church Rd DE22 6 B3
Church St Belper DE56 3 D2
Derby, Alvaston DE24 17 E4
Derby, Littleover DE23 10 B1
Derby, Rose Hill DE23 11 D1
Derby, Spondon DE21 12 B3
Holbrook DE56 5 E3
Horsley DE21 5 F3
Kilburn DE56 5 F4
Ockbrook DE72 13 E2
Church Wlk Derby DE22 7 D2
Duffield DE56 4 C1
Churchdown Cl DE21 8 A1
Circle The DE24 15 F3
City Rd DE1 11 D4
City Rd Ind Pk DE1 11 D4
Clarence Rd DE23 10 C1
Cleveland Ave DE21 12 A3
Clifford St DE24 11 E1
Clifton Dr DE3 9 F2
Clifton Rd DE22 6 C2
Clinton St DE21 11 E3
Clipstone Gdns DE21 8 A1
Close The
Derby, Allestree DE23 6 C1
Derby, Rose Hill DE23 10 B1
Cloudwood Cl DE23 10 A1
Clover Cl DE21 12 C3
Cloverdale Dr DE24 15 F1
Cloverslade DE65 14 B1
Club La DE73 18 A3
Cluster Rd DE56 2 C2
Clusters The DE56 2 C2
Co-operative St DE23 10 C1
Coach Dr DE22 6 B4
Cobden St DE22 10 B3
Cobham Cl DE24 15 E2
Cobthorn Dr DE22 6 B2
Cockayne St N DE24 16 C3
Cockayne St S DE24 16 C3
Cod Beck Cl DE24 17 E3
Coke St DE22 10 B3
Coldstream Wlk DE24 15 F2
Cole La DE72 13 E2
Coleman St DE24 16 C4
Coleraine Cl DE21 12 A2
Coleridge St
Derby, Littleover DE23 15 F3
Derby, Normanton DE23 15 F4
College Mews DE1 10 C3
Collier La DE72 13 E2
Collingham Gdns DE22 10 A3
Collis Cl DE24 16 C4
Collumbell Ave DE72 13 E3
Colombo St DE23 11 D1
Coltsfoot Dr DE24 15 F1
Columbine Cl DE21 8 A1
Colvile St DE22 10 B3
Colwell Dr DE24 17 E3
Colwyn Ave DE23 10 B1
Comfrey Cl DE23 14 C3
Commerce St DE24 16 C4
Common Piece La DE65 14 C1
Common The DE22 6 B4
Compton Cl DE24 17 E3
Coniston Ave DE21 12 C3
Coniston Cres DE21 7 E1
Connaught Rd DE22 10 B2
Consett Cl DE21 7 E1
Consort Gdns DE21 8 B2
Constable Ave DE23 10 B1
Constable Dr DE23 10 A1
Constable La DE23 10 B2
Conway Ave DE72 13 E1
Cook Cl DE56 3 F3
Cookfield DE56 3 F4
Cookham Cl DE3 9 E1
Cooper St DE22 10 B3
Coopers Cl DE72 13 E1

Cope Ct DE24 16 A3
Copes Way DE21 12 A4
Coppice Cl DE22 6 C1
Copse Gr DE23 15 D4
Corbel Cl DE21 7 F1
Corbridge Gr DE23 15 D4
Corden Ave DE3 10 A1
Corden St DE23 11 D1
Cordville Cl DE21 12 A3
Corfe Cl DE23 15 E3
Coriander Gdns DE23 15 E2
Corinium Cl DE24 17 E3
Cornflower Dr DE21 8 A2
Cornhill DE22 6 C2
Cornwall Rd DE21 11 E3
Coronation Ave
Belper DE56 3 D3
Derby DE24 17 E3
Coronation St DE23 16 A4
Coronet Ct DE21 8 B2
Coton Rd DE23 11 D1
Cotswold Cl DE23 15 E4
Cottisford Cl DE23 15 D4
Cotton La DE24 11 E1
Countisbury Dr DE21 8 A1
Court The DE24 17 D3
Courtland Dr DE24 17 D3
Courtland Gdns DE24 17 D4
Courtney Way DE56 3 E3
Coverdale Wlk DE24 17 E4
Covert The DE21 12 C2
Cowdray Cl DE24 15 E1
Cowley St DE22 10 C4
Cowper St DE24 16 A3
Cowsley Rd DE21 11 E4
Cox Green Cl DE23 14 C4
Cox Green Ct DE23 14 C4
Coxbench Rd DE21 5 F2
Coxon St DE21 12 C3
Crab Tree Hill DE21 7 E4
Crabtree Cl DE22 6 B2
Crabtree Hill DE21 6 B2
Craddock Ave DE21 12 C2
Craiglee Ct DE24 15 E2
Cranhill Cl DE23 14 C3
Crawley Rd DE24 16 C3
Crayford Rd DE24 17 D3
Crecy Cl DE22 10 B2
Crescent The
Derby, Boulton DE24 16 C3
Derby, Chaddesden DE21 11 F3
Cressbrook Way DE21 8 A2
Crest The DE22 6 C1
Crewe St DE23 10 C1
Crewton Way DE24 16 C4
Crich Ave DE23 10 B1
Crich Cir DE23 10 B1
Crich La DE56 3 D4
Crich View DE56 3 F4
Cricketers Ct DE23 15 E4
Cricklewood Rd DE22 10 A3
Cringle Mews DE21 7 F1
Croft Cl Derby DE21 12 C3
Ockbrook DE72 13 E2
Croft End DE21 7 E4
Croft La DE21 7 E2
Croft The Belper DE56 3 E1
Derby DE72 15 E4
Crofters Ct DE21 7 F1
Cromarty Cl DE24 15 F2
Cromer Cl DE3 9 E1
Cromford Dr DE3 9 F2
Cromford Rd DE21 12 A4
Cromwell Ave DE65 14 B1
Cromwell Rd DE23 10 C1
Cropton Cl DE24 17 E3
Crosby St DE22 10 B2
Cross Cl DE23 15 E4
Cross St DE22 10 B3
Crossdale Gr DE21 8 B2
Crown Mews DE22 10 C2
Crown St Derby DE22 10 C2
Duffield DE56 4 C2
Crown Terr DE56 2 C2
Crownland Dr DE73 17 D1
Crowshaw St DE24 16 A4
Croydon Wlk DE22 9 F3
Cuckmere Cl DE22 7 D3
Culworth Cl DE56 3 E2
Culworth Ct DE21 8 A1
Cumberhills Rd DE56 4 B1
Cumberland Ave DE21 11 F3
Cumberland Cres DE72 13 D1
Cumbria Wlk DE3 9 E1
Cummings St DE23 11 D1
Curborough Dr DE24 17 E3
Curlew Cl 1 DE24 15 E2
Curzon CE Prim Sch The
DE22 6 B3
Curzon Cl DE22 6 B2
Curzon Ct DE56 4 C2
Curzon La Derby DE24 17 D4
Duffield DE56 4 B2
Curzon Rd DE21 11 F4
Cut La DE1 11 D4
Cuttlebrook Cl DE23 15 F3
Cypress Wlk DE21 12 A3

Dahlia Dr DE21 8 B2
Dairy House Rd DE23 11 D1
Dalbury Wlk DE23 15 E3
Dale Ct DE56 5 F4
Dale Prim Sch DE23 10 C1
Dale Rd Dale DE21 13 D3
Derby, Alvaston DE24 17 D4
Dale Rd continued
Derby, Rose Hill DE23 10 C1
Derby, Spondon DE21 12 C3
Dale View Gdns DE56 5 F4
Dalkieth Ave DE24 16 C3
Dalley La DE56 2 B3
Dalness Ct 4 DE24 15 E2
Dalton Ave DE22 10 B2
Danebridge Cres DE21 8 A1
Darby St DE23 10 C1
Dark La DE56 5 D4
Darley Abbey Dr DE22 6 C1
Darley Gr DE1 11 D4
Darley Park Dr DE22 6 C1
Darley Park Rd DE22 6 C1
Darley St DE22 7 D1
Dartford Pl DE24 17 D3
Darwin Ave DE24 16 B2
Darwin Rd DE3 9 F2
Datchet Cl DE23 15 D4
Davenport Rd DE24 16 B4
Daventry Cl DE3 9 E2
David's Cl DE73 16 C1
Dawlish Ct DE24 17 E4
Dawsmere Cl DE21 7 E1
Daylesford Cl DE23 15 D4
Days La DE56 2 C2
Dayton Cl DE21 12 B3
Deacon Cl DE21 7 F1
Deadman's La DE24 11 E1
Dean Cl DE23 10 A1
Dean St DE22 10 C2
Deans Dr DE72 13 D1
Deborah Dr DE21 12 A4
Dee Cl DE24 15 F2
Deep Dale La
Barrow u T DE73 18 A4
Derby DE24 15 F1
Derby DE24, DE73 15 F1
Deepdale Ave DE72 13 E1
Deepdale Rd Belper DE56 3 D3
Derby DE21 12 C2
Deer Park View DE21 12 C3
Deincourt Cl DE21 13 D3
Delamere Cl DE21 8 A1
Denarth Ave DE24 16 C2
Denbigh St DE21 11 F4
Denison Gdns DE21 12 A3
Dennis Cl DE23 14 C4
Denstone Dr DE24 17 D2
Dentdale Ct DE24 17 E4
Denver Rd DE3 9 E2
Depot St DE23 11 D1
Derby City Hospl DE23 10 A1
Derby High Sch DE23 10 A1
Derby Ind Gram Sch
for Boys DE23 14 C4
Derby La DE23 15 F4
Derby Moor Com Sch
DE23 15 D4
Derby Rd Belper DE56 4 C4
Borrowash DE21, DE72 13 D1
Borrowash, Shacklecross
DE72 13 E1
Dale DE21 8 C2
Derby, Chellaston DE73 16 C1
Derby, Spondon DE21 12 B2
Duffield DE56 4 C1
Horsley DE21 5 E3
Kilburn DE56 3 F1
King's Newton DE73 19 D1
Derby Sta DE1 11 E2
Derby Trad Est DE21 11 D4
Derby Univ
(Mickleover Site) DE3 9 F2
Derbyshire Cty Cricket Gd
DE21 11 E3
Derrington Leys DE24 17 E3
Derventio Cl DE1 11 D4
Derwent Ave Belper DE56 3 D1
Borrowash DE72 13 E2
Derby DE72 7 D2
Derwent Cl DE22 7 D2
Derwent Com Sch DE21 11 E4
Derwent Dr DE24 15 E1
Derwent Rd DE21 12 B2
Derwent Rise DE21 12 C2
Derwent St DE56 2 C2
Derwent Vale DE56 2 C2
Derwent View DE56 2 C3
Devas Gdns DE21 12 B3
Devon Cl DE21 11 E3
Devonshire Ave
Borrowash DE72 13 E1
Derby DE22 6 C2
Devonshire Dr Derby DE3 9 F2
Duffield DE56 4 B1
Dewchurch Dr DE23 15 F3
Dexter St DE23 11 E1
Diamond Dr DE21 7 F2
Dickens Sq DE23 15 F4
Dickinson St DE24 11 E1
Dodburn Ct DE24 15 E2
Doles La DE65 14 B2
Dolphin Cl DE21 13 D3
Donald Hawley Way DE56 4 C2
Donegal Wlk DE21 12 A2
Donnington Cl DE23 15 F3
Donnington Dr DE23 15 F3
Dorchester Ave DE21 11 F4
Dorking Rd DE22 10 A3
Dorrien Ave DE23 16 A4
Dorset St DE21 11 E3
Douglas St DE23 11 D1
Dove Cl DE3 10 A2
Dovecote Dr DE72 13 D1
Dovecote The DE21 5 F3
Dovedale Ave DE24 17 E4
Dovedale Cres DE56 3 D3
Dovedale Ct DE56 3 D2
Dovedale Rd DE21 12 C2
Dovedale Rise DE22 6 B1
Dover Ct DE23 11 D1
Dover St DE23 11 D1
Doveridge Wlk DE23 15 E3
Dower Cl DE22 7 D1
Downham Cl DE3 9 F1
Downing Cl DE22 9 F3
Downing Rd DE21 11 E3
Downmeadow DE56 3 F4
Drage St DE1 11 D4
Draycott Dr DE3 9 E2
Draycott Rd DE72 13 E1
Drayton Ave DE22 9 F3
Dresden Cl DE3 9 E1
Drewery La DE22 10 C2
Drewry Ct DE1 10 C3
Dreyfus Cl DE21 12 C3
Drive The DE56 1 F2
Drury Ave DE21 12 B2
Dryden St DE23 15 F4
Drysdale Rd DE3 9 E2
Duesbury Cl DE24 16 C4
Duffield Bank DE56 5 D2
Duffield Rd
Derby, Allestree DE22 7 D3
Derby, Darley Abbey DE22 6 C1
Little Eaton DE21 7 D3
Duffield Sta DE56 4 C2
Dukeries La DE21 8 A1
Duluth Ave DE21 12 A4
Dulverton Ave DE24 15 E1
Dulwich Rd DE22 9 F3
Dunbar Cl DE24 15 F1
Duncan Cl DE56 3 D3
Duncan Rd DE23 15 F4
Dunedin Cl DE3 9 F2
Dunkery Ct DE21 8 A1
Dunoon Cl DE24 15 F2
Dunsmore Dr DE21 7 F1
Dunstall Park Rd DE24 16 B4
Dunvegan Cl DE24 15 E1
Durham Ave DE21 11 F3
Durley Cl DE24 17 E4
Durward Cl DE24 16 B4

Ealing Cl DE22 10 A3
Eardley Cl DE21 12 A3
Earls Cres DE21 8 A1
Earlswood Dr DE3 9 F2
East Ave DE3 9 F2
East Cl DE22 6 C1
East Cres DE56 5 E4
East Croft Ave DE23 15 E3
East Lawn DE65 14 B1
East Midlands
Nuffield Hospl DE23 14 C3
East Service Rd DE21 12 A2
Eastbrae Rd DE23 15 E4
Eastleigh Dr DE3 9 F1
Eastwood Ave DE23 10 B1
Eastwood Dr DE23 10 B1
Eaton Ave DE22 7 D3
Eaton Bank DE56 5 D1
Eaton Cl DE65 7 D3
Eaton Ct Derby DE1 10 C3
Duffield DE56 4 C1
Ecclesbourne Ave DE56 4 C2
Ecclesbourne Cl DE56 4 C2
Ecclesbourne Sch DE56 4 C2
Edale Ave
Derby, Alvaston DE24 17 D4
Derby, Mickleover DE3 9 E1
Derby, Rose Hill DE23 10 C1
Edale Cl DE22 6 B1
Edale Dr DE21 12 C2
Edale Way DE56 3 D3
Eden Rd DE21 12 A2
Eden St DE24 17 D4
Edensor Dr DE56 3 E3
Edensor Sq DE22 10 C2
Edge Hill DE73 16 C2
Edgelaw Ct 10 DE24 15 E2
Edgware Rd DE22 9 F3
Edinburgh Cres DE24 16 C2
Edith Wood Cl DE24 17 D3
Edmund Rd DE21 12 C2
Edmund's Sq DE3 14 A4
Ednaston Ave DE23 15 E3
Edward Ave DE21 12 A3
Edward St DE56 3 D2
Edwinstowe Rd DE21 8 A1
Eggesford Rd DE24 15 E1
Egmanton Cl DE21 8 A1
Eland Cl DE21 13 D3
Elgin Ave DE23 10 A1
Eliot Rd DE23 15 D4
Elizabeth Cl DE21 12 A3
Elkstone Cl DE21 8 A1
Ellastone Gdns DE24 17 D4
Ellendale Rd DE21 12 A4
Ellesmere Ave DE24 11 E1
Elm Ave DE56 3 D1
Elm Gr Derby, Allestree DE22 6 B3
Derby, Cherrytree Hill DE21 12 A3
Elm St DE72 13 D1
Elms Ave DE23 10 A1
Elms Dr DE23 10 A1
Elms St DE1 10 C4
Elmtree Ave DE24 16 A4
Elmwood Dr DE21 7 E1
Elsecar Cl DE56 3 E3
Elton Rd DE24 16 A4
Elvaston Castle DE21 17 F4
Elvaston Castle Ctry Pk
DE21 17 F3
Elvaston La DE24 17 E4
Embankment Cl DE22 9 F4
Emerald Cl DE21 8 A1
Emerson Sq DE23 15 F3
Endsleigh Gdns DE22 9 F3
Enfield Rd DE22 10 A3
Ennerdale Wlk DE21 7 E1
Ennis Cl DE21 12 B4
Enoch Stone Dr DE21 12 A2
Epping Cl DE22 9 F3
Epworth Dr DE24 17 D2
Eskdale Wlk DE24 17 E3
Essex St DE21 11 E3
Eton St DE24 11 F1
Ettrick Dr DE24 15 F1
Etwall Rd DE3 9 E1
Etwall St DE22 10 C3
Evans Ave DE22 7 D3
Evans St DE24 16 C3
Evanston Gdns DE21 12 A3
Evelyn Gr DE21 12 A3
Evergreen Cl DE21 8 A2
Evesham Cl DE21 7 F1
Excelsior Ave DE24 16 C3
Eyam Wlk DE56 3 D3
Eyes Ct DE56 4 C2
Eyrie The DE24 15 F1

Fairbourne Dr DE3 9 E2
Fairdene DE23 10 C1
Faire St DE22 10 C2
Faires Cl DE72 13 E1
Fairfax Rd DE23 10 C1
Fairfield Ave DE72 13 E2
Fairfield Rd DE23 10 C1
Fairisle Cl DE21 8 B2
Fairview Cl DE23 15 D4
Fairway Cl DE22 6 B1
Fairway Cres DE22 6 B1
Fairwood Dr DE24 17 E3
Falcon Way DE24 15 F1
Falcons Rise DE56 3 E3
Fallow Rd DE21 12 C3
Falmouth Rd DE24 17 E3
Far La DE72 13 E3
Far Laund DE56 3 D3
Farley Rd DE23 10 B1
Farm Cl DE56 3 E2
Farm Dr DE24 17 D3
Farm St DE22 10 C2
Farmhouse Rd DE24 15 F1
Farmlands La DE23 15 D3
Farnah Green Rd DE56 2 B2
Farnborough Gdns DE22 7 D2
Farncombe La DE21 7 F2
Farndale Ct DE24 17 E3
Farneworth Rd DE3 9 E1
Farnham Cl DE3 9 E1
Farningham Cl DE21 12 C3
Farnway DE22 6 C1
Farrier Gdns DE23 15 D4
Farringdon Cl DE22 9 F3
Faversham Cl DE24 16 C3
Fellowlands Way DE73 17 D1
Fellside Belper DE56 3 D2
Derby DE21 12 C3
Fenchurch Wlk DE22 10 A4
Fenton Rd DE3 9 E1
Fenwick St DE24 16 B4
Fernhill Ct DE73 17 D2
Fernilee Gdns DE21 7 D4
Fernwood Cl DE23 15 E4
Ferrers Cres DE56 4 B2
Ferrers Way DE22 6 C1
Field Cl DE72 13 D2
Field Cres DE24 17 D3
Field Dr DE24 17 D3
Field Head Way DE21 8 A2
Field La Belper DE56 2 C2
Derby, Boulton DE24 17 D3
Derby, Chaddesden DE21 12 A4
Field Rise DE23 15 E4
Field Row DE56 2 C2
Field View Cl DE24 17 D3
Fieldgate Dr DE21 7 F1
Fife St DE24 16 C4
Fincham Cl DE21 7 E1
Finchley Ave DE22 9 F3
Findern Cl Belper DE56 3 E3
Derby DE22 6 B1
Findern La DE65 14 A2
Findern St DE22 10 B3
Finmere Cl DE23 15 D4
Finningley Dr DE22 6 C1
Finsbury Ave DE22 10 A3
Finsley Wlk DE23 15 F3
Firestone DE56 2 B1
Firlawns DE56 4 B2
Firs Cres DE22 6 C2
Firs Estate Prim Sch
DE22 10 C2
Firtree Gr DE21 8 A1
Fisher La DE56 4 C2
Fisher St DE24 16 C3
Fiskerton Way DE21 8 A1
Five Lamps Ct DE1 10 C3
Flamstead St DE24 16 C3
Flat The DE56 5 F4
Flaxholme Ave DE56 4 C1
Fleet Cres DE56 2 C2
Fleet Pk DE56 3 D2
Fleet St DE23 11 D1
Fleet The DE56 2 C2
Flint St DE24 16 B3
Flood St DE72 13 E2
Folkestone Dr DE24 17 D3
Folly Rd DE22 7 D1
Ford La DE65 7 D3
Ford St Belper DE56 2 C2
Derby DE1 10 C3
Fordwells Cl DE23 15 D4
Foremark Ave DE23 15 F4
Forest Cl DE56 3 D3
Forrester Ave DE72 19 F3
Forum Cl DE24 17 E3
Fosse Cl DE72 13 E1
Foundry La DE56 4 C4
Fountains Cl DE22 7 D2
Fowler Ave DE21 12 B2
Fowler St DE22 10 C3
Fox Cl DE24 15 E1
Foxdell Way DE73 17 D1
Foxes Wlk DE22 6 C2
Foxfields Dr DE21 7 F1
Foxlands Ave DE22 6 C1
Foxley Ct DE21 8 A1
Foyle Ave DE21 12 A2
Frampton Gdns DE23 14 C3
Franchise St DE22 10 C2
Francis St DE21 11 E3
Franklyn Dr DE24 17 D3
Frazer Cl DE21 12 C3
Frederick Ave DE24 16 C3
Frederick St DE22 10 B3
Freehold St DE22 10 C2
Freeman Ave DE23 15 F3
Freemantle Rd DE3 9 F2
Freesia Cl DE3 9 F1
French La DE21 5 F3
French St DE23 10 C1
Fresco Dr DE23 14 C4
Friar Gate DE1 10 C3
Friar Gate Ct DE1 10 C3
Friar Gate House Sch DE1 10 C3
Friars Cl DE22 7 D1
Friary Ave DE24 16 C3
Fritchley Cl DE21 8 A1
Froggatt Cl DE22 7 D3
Fulbrook Rd DE23 15 D4
Fulham Rd DE22 10 A3
Fulmar Cl DE3 10 A2
Furrows Cl DE21 8 B2

Gable Ct DE3 14 C4
Gainborough Cl DE21 8 A1
Gairloch Cl DE24 15 E1
Galway Ave DE21 12 A2
Garfield Cl DE23 15 E3
Garrick St DE24 17 D4
Garry Cl DE24 15 E1
Garsdale Ct DE24 17 E3
Garth Cres DE24 17 D3
Garthorpe Ct DE21 7 F1
Gary Cl DE23 15 E3
Gascoine Dr DE21 12 B2
Gaskell Ave DE23 15 F4
Gatcombe Cl DE21 8 A1
Gayton Ave DE23 15 E3
Gayton Com Jun Sch
DE23 15 E3
Gayton Thorpe Cl DE23 14 C4
Gema Cl DE22 7 D2
George St DE56 2 C2
Gerard Cl DE21 12 C3
Gertrude Rd DE21 12 A4
Gibfield La DE56 2 C1
Gilbert Cl DE21 12 B2
Gilbert Cres DE56 4 C1
Gilbert St DE24 17 D3
Gilderdale Way DE21 8 A2
Gillamoor Ct DE24 17 E3
Gisborne Cl DE3 9 F2
Gisborne Cres DE22 6 C2
Gisborne Gn DE1 10 C3
Gladstone Cl DE73 16 C2
Gladstone Rd DE21 12 C3
Gladstone St DE23 10 C1
Glaisdale Nook DE24 17 E3
Glamis Cl DE21 8 A1
Glastonbury Rd DE24 17 E4
Glebe Rise DE23 10 B1
Glen Ave DE56 5 E4
Glen View DE56 2 C1
Glencroft Dr DE24 15 E2
Glendale Dr DE21 12 C3
Glendon Rd DE24 15 E2
Gleneagles Cl DE3 9 F1
Glenfield Cres DE3 9 E1
Glengarry Way DE24 15 F2
Glenmore Dr DE24 15 E2
Glenmoy Cl DE23 15 E4
Glenorchy Ct DE21 8 A2
Glenwood Rd DE73 19 D4
Glossop St DE24 16 A4
Gloster St DE24 11 F1
Goathland Rd DE24 15 E1
Gold La DE22 9 F4
Goldcrest Dr DE21 12 C3
Golders Green Wlk DE22 10 A3
Golf La DE56 4 C3
Goodale St DE23 11 D1
Goodrington Rd DE21 8 B2
Goods Rd DE56 2 C1
Goods Yd DE56 2 C1
Goodsmoor Rd DE23 15 F3
Goodwin's La DE56 2 B1
Goodwood Dr DE24 17 E3
Gordon Rd Borrowash DE72 13 D1
Derby DE23 10 C2
Gorse Cl DE23 15 E3
Gorses DE56 2 B4
Gorsey Cl DE56 2 C3
Gorsty Leys DE65 14 B1
Gosforth Rd DE24 16 C4
Grafham Cl DE73 17 D2
Grafton St DE23 10 C1

Grampian Prim Sch DE24 .... 15 E2
Grampian Way DE24 .... 15 F2
Grandstand Rd DE21 .... 11 E3
Grange Ave DE72 .... 15 F4
Grange Rd DE24 .... 17 D3
Grange St DE23 .... 11 D1
Grangewood Dr DE56 .... 5 D4
Grant Ave DE21 .... 12 A3
Grantham Ave DE21 .... 7 F1
Granville Cl DE56 .... 4 C2
Granville St DE1 .... 10 C3
Grasmere Ave DE21 .... 12 C3
Grasmere Cres DE24 .... 15 F2
Grassthorpe Cl DE21 .... 8 A1
Gravel Pit La DE21 .... 12 C2
Grayling St DE23 .... 11 D1
Great Northern Rd DE1 .... 10 C3
Greatorex Ave DE24 .... 16 C3
Green Ave DE73 .... 17 D1
Green La Barrow u T DE73 .... 18 A3
Belper DE56 .... 2 C2
Burnaston DE65 .... 14 A2
Derby, Alvaston DE24 .... 17 E4
Ockbrook DE72 .... 13 E3
Green Pk DE22 .... 10 A3
Green The Belper DE56 .... 3 D3
Derby, Allestree DE22 .... 6 B1
Derby, Mickleover DE74 .... 9 E1
Findern DE65 .... 14 B1
Green Way DE65 .... 14 B1
Greenacres DE23 .... 15 D4
Greenbank DE21 .... 12 B2
Greenburn Cl DE23 .... 15 E3
Greenfell Ave DE23 .... 15 F3
Greenfields Ave DE23 .... 15 D4
Greenfinch Cl DE21 .... 12 C3
Greenland Ave DE22 .... 10 A3
Greenside Ct DE3 .... 9 E1
Greenway Cl DE72 .... 13 D2
Greenwich Dr N DE22 .... 10 B3
Greenwich Dr S DE22 .... 10 A3
Greenwood Ave DE21 .... 11 F4
Greenwood Cl DE24 .... 16 B3
Gregory Wlk DE23 .... 14 C4
Gregorys Way DE56 .... 3 E3
Gresham Rd DE24 .... 16 B4
Griffin Cl DE24 .... 16 C4
Grimshaw Ave DE24 .... 17 D4
Grindlow Rd DE21 .... 12 A4
Grosvenor St DE24 .... 16 B4
Grove Cl DE72 .... 17 F2
Grove The DE72 .... 9 F1
Grovebury Dr DE23 .... 15 E3
Groves Nook DE73 .... 16 C1
Gurney Ave DE23 .... 15 E3
Gypsy La DE72 .... 13 F1

Haddon Cl DE22 .... 6 B2
Haddon Dr
Derby, Allestree DE3 .... 6 B2
Derby, Mickleover DE3 .... 9 F2
Derby, Spondon DE21 .... 12 C2
Little Eaton DE21 .... 5 E1
Haddon St DE23 .... 10 C1
Hagg La DE56 .... 1 E1
Haig St DE24 .... 16 C4
Hailsham Cl DE3 .... 9 E2
Haines Cl DE24 .... 15 F2
Halifax Cl DE65 .... 7 E1
Hall Dyke DE21 .... 12 B3
Hall Farm Rd DE56 .... 4 C1
Hall Leys La DE73 .... 19 E1
Hall Pk DE73 .... 18 A3
Hall St DE24 .... 17 D4
Halstock Dr DE24 .... 17 E4
Hambledon Dr DE24 .... 15 E1
Hamblin Cres DE24 .... 15 F2
Hamilton Cl DE3 .... 9 F2
Hamilton Rd
Derby, Rose Hill DE23 .... 10 C1
Derby, Spondon DE21 .... 12 C3
Hampden St DE23 .... 16 A4
Hampshire Rd DE21 .... 11 E4
Hampstead Dr DE22 .... 10 A3
Hampton Cl DE21 .... 12 C3
Hanbury Rd DE21 .... 11 F3
Handel St DE24 .... 16 B4
Handford Ct DE22 .... 10 B3
Handford St DE22 .... 10 B3
Hanover Sq DE22 .... 10 A3
Hanslynn DE72 .... 17 F2
Hanwell Way DE22 .... 10 A3
Hardhurst Rd DE24 .... 17 D3
Hardwick Ave DE22 .... 6 B2
Hardwick Dr DE3 .... 9 F1
Hardwick Inf & Jun Schs
DE23 .... 11 D1
Hardwick St DE24 .... 16 B4
Harebell Cl DE21 .... 8 A2
Harepit Cl DE24 .... 17 D3
Harewood Rd DE22 .... 6 B2
Hargrave Ave DE72 .... 13 E3
Harlech Cl DE21 .... 13 D3
Harlesden Ave DE22 .... 10 A4
Harlow Cl DE24 .... 16 C2
Harpswell Cl DE22 .... 6 C1
Harpur Ave DE73 .... 15 D4
Harrier Rd DE56 .... 3 E3
Harrier Way DE24 .... 15 F2
Harriet St DE23 .... 11 D2
Harringay Gdns DE22 .... 10 B3
Harrington Ave DE72 .... 13 E1
Harrington Rd DE23 .... 10 B1
Harrington St
Derby, Allenton DE24 .... 16 C3
Derby, Normanton DE23 .... 16 A4
Harrison St DE22 .... 10 C2
Harrogate Cres DE21 .... 7 E1
Harrow St DE24 .... 11 F1
Hartington Way DE3 .... 9 E1
Hartland Dr DE23 .... 15 F3
Hartshorne Rd DE23 .... 15 E3
Harvest Way DE21 .... 8 B2
Harvey Rd DE24 .... 16 C3
Hasgill Cl DE21 .... 8 B2
Haslam's La DE22 .... 7 D1
Haslemere Ct DE23 .... 11 D1
Hassop Rd DE21 .... 12 A4
Hastings St DE23 .... 11 D1
Hatchmere Cl DE21 .... 8 A1
Hatfield Rd DE24 .... 16 C3
Hathern Cl DE23 .... 15 F3
Hathersage Ave DE23 .... 15 F4
Havelock Rd DE23 .... 16 A4
Haven Baulk Ave DE23 .... 14 C4
Haven Baulk La DE23 .... 14 C4
Haven Ct DE24 .... 17 E3
Hawke St DE22 .... 10 B3
Hawkshead Ave DE21 .... 7 E1
Hawthorn Ave DE24 .... 17 D4
Hawthorn Cr DE65 .... 14 B1
Hawthorn St DE24 .... 16 B4
Hawthorne Ave DE72 .... 13 E1
Hawthorne Cl DE56 .... 3 F1
Hawthorns The
Belper DE56 .... 3 E3
Little Eaton DE21 .... 7 E4
Hawtrey Gdns DE24 .... 17 D3
Haydn Rd DE21 .... 11 F4
Haydock Park Rd DE24 .... 16 C4
Hayes Ave DE72 .... 15 E4
Hayes The DE65 .... 14 B1
Hayfield Cl DE56 .... 3 D3
Hayley Croft DE56 .... 4 C1
Haywood Cl DE24 .... 17 D3
Hazel Ave DE23 .... 15 E3
Hazel Cl DE65 .... 14 C1
Hazel Dr DE21 .... 13 D3
Hazel Gr DE56 .... 4 C2
Hazeldene Cl DE56 .... 4 C3
Hazelwood Hill DE56 .... 4 B4
Hazelwood Rd Derby DE21 .... 11 F4
Duffield DE56 .... 4 B3
Hazelwood DE56 .... 4 B3
Headingley Ct DE23 .... 15 E4
Heath Ave DE23 .... 10 B1
Heath Ct DE24 .... 15 F2
Heath La DE65 .... 14 B1
Heathcote Cl DE24 .... 17 E3
Heather Cl DE24 .... 15 E1
Heather Cres DE72 .... 15 E3
Heavygate La DE56 .... 1 F4
Hebden Cl DE23 .... 14 C3
Hebrides Cl DE24 .... 15 E2
Hedgebank Ct DE21 .... 8 B2
Hedgerow Gdns DE21 .... 8 B2
Hedingham Way DE3 .... 14 B4
Heigham Cl DE24 .... 16 B2
Helston Cl DE24 .... 17 D3
Hemlock Cl DE21 .... 8 A2
Hendon Way DE22 .... 10 A3
Henley Gn DE22 .... 9 F3
Herbert Strutt Prim Sch
DE56 .... 2 C1
Hereford Rd DE21 .... 11 E4
Hermitage Ave DE72 .... 13 E1
Hermitage Ct DE21 .... 8 A1
Heron Way DE3 .... 10 A1
Heronswood Dr DE21 .... 12 B3
Hexham Wlk DE21 .... 7 F1
Heydon Cl DE56 .... 3 D3
Heyworth St DE22 .... 10 B3
Hickling Cl DE24 .... 16 B2
High Edge Dr DE56 .... 3 F4
High Edge Mews DE56 .... 3 D3
High Pavement DE56 .... 3 D2
High St Belper DE56 .... 3 D2
Derby DE73 .... 17 D1
High View Sch & Tech Ctr
DE21 .... 7 F1
Highbury Cl DE22 .... 9 F3
Highcliff La DE56 .... 1 D2
Highfield Cotts DE21 .... 11 F3
Highfield Gdns DE22 .... 10 C4
Highfield La DE21 .... 11 F3
Highfield Mews DE21 .... 11 F3
Highfield Rd Belper DE56 .... 2 C1
Derby, Little Chester DE22 .... 10 C4
Derby, Littleover DE23 .... 15 E4
Kilburn DE56 .... 5 F4
Little Eaton DE21 .... 7 E4
Highgate Gn DE22 .... 10 A3
Highgrove Dr DE73 .... 16 C1
Highwood Ave DE56 .... 3 E1
Hilary Cl DE56 .... 3 F3
Hilderstone Cl DE24 .... 17 E3
Hill Cl Derby DE21 .... 12 C2
Turnditch DE56 .... 1 D1
Hill Crest Rd DE21 .... 11 E4
Hill Cross Ave DE23 .... 15 E4
Hill Cross Dr DE23 .... 15 D4
Hill Nook Cl DE73 .... 17 D1
Hill Park Cl DE23 .... 10 A1
Hill Rise Cl DE23 .... 15 E4
Hill Sq The DE22 .... 7 D1
Hill The DE22 .... 7 D1
Hill Top DE21 .... 7 F2
Hill View DE56 .... 4 B2
Hill View Gr DE21 .... 12 C3
Hillcreste Dr DE73 .... 16 C2
Hillcroft Dr DE72 .... 13 E2
Hillside DE65 .... 14 B1
Hillside Ave DE21 .... 12 A3
Hillside Cres DE21 .... 12 C2
Hillside Rd DE21 .... 12 C2
Hillside Rise DE56 .... 2 C1
Hillsway
Derby, Chellaston DE73 .... 16 C2
Derby, Littleover DE23 .... 10 A1
Hilton Cl DE3 .... 9 E1
Hindscarth Cres DE3 .... 9 F1
Hob Hill DE56 .... 4 A4
Hobart Cl DE3 .... 9 F1
Hobkirk Dr DE24 .... 15 F1
Hodge Beck Cl DE24 .... 17 E3
Hodthorpe Cl DE21 .... 8 A1
Holborn Dr DE22 .... 10 A4
Holbrook CE Prim Sch DE56 . 5 E4
Holbrook Rd Belper DE56 .... 2 C1
Derby DE24 .... 17 D3
Holcombe St DE23 .... 11 D1
Holderness Cl DE24 .... 15 E1
Hollies Rd DE22 .... 6 B2
Hollington Cl DE21 .... 11 F4
Hollis St DE24 .... 17 D4
Hollow The
Derby, Littleover DE74 .... 15 E4
Derby, Mickleover DE3 .... 14 B4
Holloway Rd Derby DE24 .... 16 C3
Duffield DE56 .... 4 C2
Hollowood Ave DE23 .... 15 E4
Holly Brook Way DE23 .... 14 C3
Holly Bush La DE56 .... 5 D3
Holly Ct DE3 .... 9 E1
Hollybrook Way DE23 .... 14 C3
Hollymoor Dr DE73 .... 16 C1
Holm Ave DE21 .... 7 D4
Holme La DE21 .... 12 B2
Holmes St DE23 .... 11 D1
Holmesfield Dr DE3 .... 9 F1
Holmfield DE23 .... 15 F4
Holmoak Cl DE21 .... 8 A2
Holt Ave DE24 .... 17 E3
Holtlands Dr DE24 .... 16 C3
Holyhead Dr DE21 .... 8 A2
Holyrood Cl DE21 .... 13 D3
Home Farm Cl DE72 .... 13 E3
Home Farm Dr DE22 .... 7 D2
Honeycroft Cl DE56 .... 3 D1
Hope Ave DE3 .... 9 E1
Hopetoun St DE23 .... 16 A4
Hopping Hill DE56 .... 4 C4
Hopping Hill Terr E DE56 .... 5 D4
Hopping Hill Terr W DE56 .... 5 D4
Hopton Cl DE21 .... 8 A1
Hopwell Sch DE72 .... 13 F3
Hornbeam Cl DE21 .... 7 F1
Horncastle Rd DE21 .... 7 E1
Hornsea Rd DE21 .... 7 E1
Horsley CE Prim Sch DE21 .... 5 F3
Horsley Cres DE56 .... 5 E4
Horsley La DE21 .... 5 F2
Horsley Rd Horsley DE21 .... 5 F3
Kilburn DE56 .... 5 F3
Horton St DE23 .... 11 E1
Horwood Ave DE23 .... 10 B1
Hospital La DE3 .... 14 A4
Houghton Ct DE21 .... 7 F1
Hoult St DE22 .... 10 B2
Hounslow Rd DE22 .... 10 A3
Houston Cl DE21 .... 12 A3
Hoveton Cl DE24 .... 16 B2
Howard St DE23 .... 10 C1
Howden Cl DE3 .... 9 E1
Howe St DE22 .... 10 B3
Howth Cl DE21 .... 12 A2
Hoylake Ct DE3 .... 9 E2
Hoylake Dr DE3 .... 9 E2
Hoyland Ct DE56 .... 3 F3
Hubert Shaw Cl DE24 .... 16 C2
Hucklow Ct DE21 .... 8 A2
Hulland View DE22 .... 6 B1
Humber Cl DE24 .... 17 E3
Humbleton Dr DE22 .... 10 A3
Hunter Dr DE56 .... 5 F4
Hunter Rd DE56 .... 3 E3
Hunters Croft DE24 .... 15 F1
Huntingdon Gn DE21 .... 11 E3
Huntley Ave DE21 .... 12 C3
Hutton St DE24 .... 16 C3
Hyde Park Rd DE22 .... 10 A3

Ibsley Cl DE24 .... 17 E3
Ilford Rd DE22 .... 10 A3
Ilford Wlk DE22 .... 10 A3
Imperial Ct DE22 .... 6 B3
Industrial St DE23 .... 11 D1
Ingham Dr DE3 .... 14 B4
Ingle Cl DE21 .... 12 C3
Ingle's Channel DE56 .... 2 C2
Ingleby Ave DE23 .... 15 F4
Inglewood Ave DE3 .... 9 E2
Ingliston Cl DE24 .... 17 E3
Inn La DE22 .... 6 A4
Instow Dr DE23 .... 15 E3
Inveraray Cl DE24 .... 15 F2
Invernia Cl DE23 .... 15 F3
Iona Cl DE24 .... 15 F2
Irvine Cl DE24 .... 15 E2
Irving Pl DE24 .... 16 C4
Islay Rd DE24 .... 15 F2
Isleworth Dr DE22 .... 9 F3
Ismay Rd DE21 .... 11 F3
Ivy Ct DE3 .... 9 E1
Ivy House Specl Sch DE23 .. 11 E1
Ivy Sq DE23 .... 11 E1
Ivybridge Cl DE21 .... 8 B2

Jacksdale Cl DE22 .... 6 B1
Jackson Ave DE3 .... 10 A1
Jackson St DE22 .... 10 C2
Jackson's La DE56 .... 3 E4
Jacksons La DE56 .... 4 C4
James Cl DE1 .... 10 C3
Jarvey's La DE22 .... 9 F4
Jarvis Rd DE24 .... 15 F1
Jasmine Cl DE21 .... 12 A3
Jebb's La DE56 .... 1 D4
Jedburgh Cl DE24 .... 15 F1
Jefferson Pl DE24 .... 16 C4
Jemison Cl DE23 .... 14 C4
Jenny's Ct DE56 .... 3 E3
Jesses La DE56 .... 2 B4
Jessop Dr DE24 .... 15 F1
Jodrell Ave DE56 .... 3 E2
John Berrysford Cl DE21 .... 11 F3
John F Kennedy Gdns DE21 12 B3
John Lombe Dr DE1 .... 11 D4
John O'Gaunts Way DE56 .... 3 E2
Johnson Ave DE24 .... 16 C4
Joseph St Belper DE56 .... 2 C2
Derby DE23 .... 11 D1
Jubalton Cl DE24 .... 16 C3
Jubilee Ct DE56 .... 3 D1
Jubilee Rd DE24 .... 16 C2
Junction St DE1 .... 10 C2

Katrine Wlk DE24 .... 15 F2
Kean Pl DE24 .... 16 C4
Keats Ave DE23 .... 10 A1
Kedleston Cl DE22 .... 6 B1
Kedleston Old Rd DE22 .... 10 B4
Kedleston Rd Derby DE22 .... 6 A3
Quarndon DE22 .... 6 A3
Kegworth Ave DE23 .... 15 E3
Keldholme La DE24 .... 17 E3
Kelmoor Rd DE24 .... 17 D4
Kemble Pl DE24 .... 16 C4
Kempton Park Rd DE24 .... 16 B4
Kendal Wlk DE21 .... 7 E1
Kendon Ave DE23 .... 15 F3
Kendray Cl DE56 .... 3 E3
Kenilworth Ave DE23 .... 15 F4
Kennedy Cl DE21 .... 12 A4
Kensal Rise DE22 .... 10 A3
Kent St DE21 .... 11 F4
Kernel Cl DE23 .... 15 D4
Kerry St DE21 .... 11 F4
Kerry's Yd DE56 .... 5 F4
Kershope Dr DE21 .... 8 A2
Kestrels Croft DE24 .... 15 F2
Keswick Ave DE23 .... 15 F3
Kevin Cl DE21 .... 12 A4
Kew Gdns DE22 .... 10 A3
Keyhaven Cl DE21 .... 11 E4
Keynsham Cl DE24 .... 16 C4
Kibworth Cl DE21 .... 12 A4
Kilburn Inf & Jun Schs DE56 . 5 F4
Kilburn La DE56 .... 3 F2
Kilburn Rd DE56 .... 3 E2
Kilburn Toll Bar DE56 .... 3 F1
Kildare Rd DE21 .... 12 A2
Killingworth Ave DE24 .... 15 F2
Killis La Belper DE56 .... 3 E1
Holbrook DE56 .... 5 E4
Kilnsey Ct DE23 .... 14 C3
Kimberley Rd DE72 .... 13 D1
Kinder Wlk DE22 .... 10 C2
King St Belper DE56 .... 2 C2
Duffield DE56 .... 4 C2
King's Mills La DE72 .... 19 F3
Kingfisher Wlk DE24 .... 15 F1
Kings Croft DE22 .... 6 C2
Kings Dr DE3 .... 10 A1
Kingsbury Rd DE22 .... 10 A3
Kingsclere Ave DE21 .... 8 A1
Kingsland Cl DE21 .... 7 F1
Kingsley Rd DE22 .... 6 B2
Kingsley St DE24 .... 15 F3
Kingsmead Ind Est DE22 .... 10 B3
Kingsmuir Rd DE3 .... 9 E2
Kingston St DE1 .... 10 C4
Kingsway DE22 .... 10 A3
Kingsway Hospl DE3 .... 10 A2
Kingsway Ind Est DE22 .... 10 B3
Kingsway Park Cl DE22 .... 10 B3
Kingsway Ret Pk DE22 .... 10 B3
Kingswood Ave DE56 .... 3 E3
Kinross Ave DE21 .... 11 E4
Kintyre Dr 11 DE24 .... 15 E2
Kipling Dr DE3 .... 9 E1
Kirk Dale Ave DE21 .... 12 C2
Kirk Leys Ave N DE21 .... 12 C2
Kirk Leys Ave S DE21 .... 12 C2
Kirk St DE1 .... 11 D4
Kirk's La DE56 .... 3 D2
Kirkistown Cl DE24 .... 17 E3
Kirkland Way 13 DE24 .... 15 E2
Kirkstead Cl DE21 .... 8 A1
Kitchener Ave DE23 .... 15 F4
Knights Cl DE24 .... 15 F1
Knightsbridge DE22 .... 10 A3
Knoll Cl DE23 .... 15 D4
Knowl Ave DE56 .... 2 C3
Knutsford Gn DE21 .... 7 E1
Kyle Gr DE21 .... 8 A2
Kynance Cl DE24 .... 17 E3

Laburnum Cres DE22 .... 6 B2
Laburnum Gr DE22 .... 10 A3
Ladbroke Gdns DE22 .... 9 F3
Lady Mantle Cl DE73 .... 16 C1
Ladybank Rd DE3 .... 9 E1
Ladybower Rd DE21 .... 12 C2
Ladycroft Paddock DE22 .... 6 C2
Ladygrove Cotts DE23 .... 11 D2
Ladysmith Rd DE72 .... 13 D1
Ladywell Ct DE56 .... 3 D2
Ladywood Ave DE56 .... 3 D3
Lake Dr DE23 .... 15 F4
Lakeside Dr DE23 .... 15 D4
Lambhouse La DE56 .... 1 F3
Lambley Dr DE22 .... 6 B1
Lambourn Ct DE22 .... 7 D2
Lambourn Dr DE22 .... 7 D2
Lambrook Cl DE3 .... 9 E1
Lampeter Cl DE21 .... 8 A1
Lanark St DE21 .... 11 F4
Lancaster Wlk DE21 .... 13 D3
Lander La DE56 .... 3 D2
Lang Rd DE24 .... 16 C3
Langdale Dr DE21 .... 7 E1
Langford Rd DE3 .... 9 E2
Langley Rd DE21 .... 12 C2
Langley St DE22 .... 10 B3
Langsett Dr DE73 .... 17 D1
Lanscombe Park Rd DE22 .... 6 C1
Lansing Gdns DE21 .... 12 A3
Lapwing Cl DE24 .... 15 F1
Larch Cl DE22 .... 6 B2
Larges St DE1 .... 10 C3
Lark Cl DE23 .... 15 E3
Larkhill Cres DE24 .... 15 F2
Larkin Cl DE24 .... 16 A3
Larkspur Ct DE21 .... 8 A2
Lashley Cl DE21 .... 7 F1
Lathbury Cl DE21 .... 7 E1
Lathkill Ave DE24 .... 17 E4
Lathkill Rd DE21 .... 11 F4
Latimer Cl DE23 .... 14 C4
Latimer St DE24 .... 16 B3
Latrigg Cl DE3 .... 9 F1
Lauder Cl DE24 .... 15 F1
Launceston Rd DE24 .... 17 D3
Laund Ave DE56 .... 3 D3
Laund Cl DE56 .... 3 D3
Laund Hill DE56 .... 3 D3
Laund Nook DE56 .... 3 D3
Laurie Pl DE24 .... 16 C4
Lavender Row DE22 .... 6 C1
Lawn Ave DE65 .... 6 B1
Lawn Heads Ave DE23 .... 10 B1
Lawn Prim Sch DE22 .... 6 B1
Lawnlea Cl DE23 .... 15 F3
Lawnside DE21 .... 12 C3
Lawnswood Cl DE23 .... 15 E4
Lawrence Ave DE21 .... 12 A4
Lawrence St DE23 .... 15 F4
Lea Cl DE22 .... 6 C2
Lea Dr
Derby, Chaddesden DE21 .... 11 F3
Derby, Mickleover DE3 .... 9 F2
Leacroft Rd DE23 .... 11 D1
Leafenden Cl DE22 .... 7 D2
Leafgreen La DE23 .... 15 E3
Leake St DE22 .... 10 B3
Leamington Cl DE23 .... 10 B1
Leander Cl DE23 .... 15 E4
Leaper St DE1 .... 10 C3
Leawood Gdns DE21 .... 8 A2
Leche Cft DE56 .... 3 E2
Ledbury Chase DE24 .... 15 E1
Ledbury Pl DE21 .... 7 E1
Lee Farm Cl DE73 .... 16 C1
Lees Brook Com Sch DE21 . 12 A4
Lees The DE24 .... 17 E3
Leeway DE21 .... 12 B2
Leicester St DE22 .... 10 C2
Leman St DE22 .... 10 C2
Lens Rd DE22 .... 6 B1
Lenton Ave DE21 .... 11 F3
Leominster Dr DE21 .... 8 A1
Leslie Cl DE23 .... 14 C4
Leven Cl DE24 .... 15 F1
Leveret Cl DE73 .... 17 D1
Lewis St DE23 .... 10 C1
Lewiston Rd DE21 .... 12 A3
Lexington Rd DE21 .... 12 B3
Leycote Way DE56 .... 3 D3
Leyland Ct DE1 .... 10 C4
Leyland Gdns DE1 .... 10 C4
Leyland St DE1 .... 10 C4
Leylands DE22 .... 10 C4
Leys Ct DE56 .... 3 E2
Leys Field Gdns DE73 .... 17 D1
Leys The DE21 .... 5 E1
Leytonstone Dr DE22 .... 10 A3
Lichfield Dr DE24 .... 17 D4
Lidgate Cl DE3 .... 9 E1
Lilac Ave DE22 .... 10 A3
Lilac Cl DE24 .... 17 D3
Lilac Way DE22 .... 6 B1
Lilian Prime Cl DE24 .... 17 D4
Lilley St DE24 .... 17 D3
Lime Ave
Derby, Breadsall Hilltop DE21 .... 7 E1
Duffield DE56 .... 4 C3
Lime Cres DE56 .... 3 D1
Lime Gr DE21 .... 12 A3
Lime La Derby DE21 .... 8 A2
Morley DE7 .... 8 B3
Lime Wlk DE23 .... 10 B1
Limedale Ave DE21 .... 8 A2
Limerick Rd DE21 .... 12 A2
Limes Ave DE3 .... 9 E1
Linacres Dr DE73 .... 17 D1
Lincoln Ave DE24 .... 17 D4
Lincoln Gn DE73 .... 16 C1
Lindford Cl DE21 .... 7 F2
Lindisfarne Cl 8 DE24 .... 15 E2
Lindon Dr DE24 .... 17 E3
Lindrick Cl DE3 .... 9 F1
Lindsey Cl DE21 .... 11 F3
Lingfield Rise DE3 .... 9 E2
Links Cl DE24 .... 15 F2
Linnet Cl DE21 .... 12 C3
Liskeard Dr DE22 .... 6 B2

Lismore Ct 5 DE24 15 E2
Lister Cl DE3 10 A2
Liston Dr DE22 10 C4
Litchurch La DE24 11 E1
Little Bridge St DE1 10 C3
Little Eaton Prim Sch
DE21 7 E4
Little Longstone Cl DE3 9 F1
Little Meadow Rd DE73 17 D1
Little Woodbury Dr DE23 14 C3
Littledale Cl DE21 8 B2
Littleover Com Sch DE23 14 C4
Littleover Cres DE23 10 B1
Littleover La DE23 15 F4
Litton Cl DE56 3 D3
Litton Dr DE21 12 C2
Liverpool St DE21 11 F4
Livingstone Rd DE23 10 C1
Lloyd St DE22 10 B3
Lochinvar Cl DE21 12 C2
Lockington Cl DE73 16 C1
Locko Ct DE21 12 B3
Locko Rd Dale DE21 12 C4
Derby DE21 12 C4
Lockwood Rd DE22 6 B2
Lodge Cl DE56 4 C2
Lodge Dr DE56 2 C3
Lodge La
Derby, Spondon DE21 12 B2
Shottle DE56 1 E4
Lodge Way DE3 9 E1
Lombard St DE22 9 F3
Lomond Ave DE24 15 F1
London Rd DE24 11 E1
Long Bridge La DE24 16 B4
Long Row DE56 2 C2
Long Row Prim Sch
DE56 2 C3
Longford Cl DE22 6 B1
Longford St DE22 10 C4
Longlands La DE65 14 B1
Longley La DE21 12 B3
Longstock Cl DE21 7 F1
Longstone Rise DE56 3 D3
Longthorpe Cl DE23 15 D4
Longwalls La DE56 2 B3
Lonsdale Pl DE22 10 B2
Lord St DE24 16 B3
Lorne St DE22 10 C2
Lorraine Cl DE24 16 C2
Loscoe Rd DE21 8 A1
Lothian Pl DE21 11 F4
Lothlorien Cl DE23 15 D4
Loudon St DE23 11 D2
Lousie Greaves La DE21 12 C3
Louvain Rd DE23 10 B1
Lowe St DE24 16 C3
Lower Dale Rd DE23 10 C1
Lower Gn DE65 14 B1
Lower Hall Cl DE56 5 E3
Lower Rd DE22 9 F4
Lowes La DE73 18 B4
Lowlands Rd DE56 3 D2
Loxley Cl DE21 8 A1
Loxton Ct DE3 9 E2
Loyne Cl DE24 15 F1
Luccombe Dr DE24 17 E3
Lucerne Rd DE21 8 B2
Ludgate Wlk DE22 9 F3
Ludlow Cl DE21 12 C3
Lulworth Cl DE23 15 E3
Lumb La DE56 2 A2
Lundie Cl DE24 15 E1
Lupin Cl DE21 8 B2
Lychgate Cl DE21 7 E1
Lydstep Cl DE21 8 B1
Lyndhurst Gr DE21 12 A3
Lyndhurst St DE23 11 D1
Lynton St DE22 10 C2
Lynwood Rd DE24 15 F2
Lytham Cl DE21 7 E1
Lyttelton St DE22 10 B3

Macaulay St DE24 16 A3
Mackenzie St DE22 10 B3
Mackworth Tertiary Coll
DE22 10 A3
Macready Pl DE24 16 C4
Macworth Rd DE1 10 C3
Madeley Ct DE3 9 E1
Madeley St DE23 11 D1
Madison Ave DE21 11 F4
Maidstone Dr DE24 16 C3
Maidwell Cl DE56 3 E3
Main Ave DE22 6 C3
Main St Findern DE65 14 B1
Melbourne DE73 19 E1
Weston-on-T DE72 19 F3
Maine Dr DE21 12 A3
Makeney Rd Belper DE56 5 D3
Duffield DE56 4 C1
Holbrook DE56 5 E3
Malcolm Gr DE23 14 C4
Malcolm St DE23 11 D1
Malham Rd DE23 14 C3
Malin Cl DE24 17 D3
Maltby Cl DE22 6 C1
Malton Pl DE21 7 E1
Malvern Cl DE3 9 E2
Malvern Way DE21 7 E1
Manchester St DE22 10 B3
Manifold Dr DE24 17 D4
Manor Ave DE23 10 B2
Manor Ct DE73 18 A3
Manor Park Ct DE3 10 A2
Manor Park Way DE3 10 A2
Manor Pk DE72 13 D1
Manor Rd Belper DE56 2 C2
Borrowash DE72 13 D1
Derby, California DE23 10 B1
Derby, Chellaston DE73 16 C1
Mansfield Rd DE1 11 D4
Maple Ave DE23 15 E3
Maple Dr Belper DE56 3 D1
Derby, Boulton DE24 17 D3
Derby, Chellaston DE73 17 D1
Maple Gr DE72 6 B3
Mapleton Ave DE21 7 F1
Marchington Cl DE22 6 C1
Marcus St DE1 11 D4
Maree Cl DE24 15 F2
Marfleet Cl DE3 9 E2
Margaret Ave DE21 11 F3
Margreave Rd DE21 11 F4
Marigold Cl DE21 8 A2
Marina Dr
Derby, Allenton DE24 16 C3
Derby, Spondon DE21 12 B3
Marjorie Rd DE21 11 F4
Mark's Cl DE23 15 E3
Markeaton La DE22 10 A4
Markeaton Prim Sch
DE22 10 C4
Markeaton St DE22 10 C3
Market Pl DE56 3 D2
Markham Ct DE21 7 F1
Marlborough Dr DE56 3 E3
Marlborough Rd DE24 16 B4
Marsden Cl DE56 4 C2
Marsden St DE24 16 C4
Marsh La DE56 3 D3
Marsh Lane Cres DE56 3 D2
Marshaw Cl DE3 9 F1
Marshgreen Cl DE24 17 E3
Marston Cl Belper DE56 3 E3
Derby DE23 15 E3
Martin Dr DE21 12 A4
Martindale Ct DE56 3 E3
Maryland Rd DE21 12 A3
Marylebone Cres DE22 10 A3
Masefield Ave DE23 15 F4
Matlock Rd Belper DE56 2 C4
Derby DE21 7 F1
Matthew St DE24 16 C3
Matthew Way DE23 14 C4
Max Rd DE21 11 F4
Maxwell Ave DE22 10 B4
May St DE22 10 C2
Mayfair Cres DE22 9 F3
Mayfield Rd DE21 11 F4
Maylands DE72 13 D1
Maypole La DE23 14 C4
McGough Mews DE24 16 A3
Mead Cl DE24 15 F2
Meadow Cl Derby DE21 12 C2
Findern DE65 14 B1
Meadow Ct DE56 2 C2
Meadow Farm Com
Prim Sch DE21 12 A2
Meadow La DE21 11 F3
Meadow Nook DE24 17 E3
Meadow Rd DE24 11 F1
Meadow Vale DE56 4 B2
Meadow View Cl DE21 8 A2
Meadow Way DE73 17 D1
Meadowgrass Cl DE23 15 D3
Meadowlark Gr DE21 8 A1
Meadows Croft DE56 4 B2
Meadows Ind Est The
DE21 11 E3
Meadows Prim Sch The
DE56 4 B2
Mear Dr DE72 13 D1
Meath Ave DE21 12 A2
Medina Cl DE24 17 E3
Medway Dr DE22 7 D3
Meerbrook Cl DE21 8 A1
Megaloughton La DE21 12 B2
Melandra Ct DE22 10 C2
Melbourn Cl DE22 4 C2
Melbourne Cl Belper DE56 3 D1
Derby, Allestree DE3 6 B1
Derby, Mickleover DE3 9 F2
Melbreak Cl DE3 9 F1
Melfort Cl DE24 15 F1
Mellor St DE24 16 C3
Mellor's La DE56 5 E3
Melrose Cl DE24 15 F1
Melton Ave DE73 15 E3
Memorial Rd DE22 6 B2
Mendip Ct DE21 7 F1
Menin Rd DE22 6 B1
Mercaston Rd DE21 11 F4
Merchant Ave DE21 12 B2
Merchant St DE22 10 C3
Mercian Mews DE21 12 B2
Merlin Cl DE56 3 E3
Merlin Gn DE24 15 E2
Merridale Rd DE23 15 E4
Merrill Coll DE24 16 C2
Merrill Lower Sch DE24 16 C3
Merrill Way DE24 16 B3
Merrybower Cl DE24 15 E2
Merthyr Ct DE21 8 A1
Metcalfe Cl DE24 17 D4
Meteor Ctr The DE21 7 E1
Meynell Ct DE22 6 B1
Meynell St DE23 10 C1
Michelle Cl DE24 15 E2
Michigan Cl DE21 12 B3
Micklecroft Gdns DE23 14 C4
Mickleover Prim Sch DE3 9 E1
Mickleross Cl DE3 9 E2
Middlebeck Cl DE73 16 C1
Middleton Ave DE23 10 B1
Middleton St DE23 11 D1
Midway DE22 6 C1
Milbank Cl DE3 9 F3
Milburn Gdns DE21 8 A2
Milbury Cl DE21 7 F1
Mile Ash La DE22 6 C1
Milford Prim Sch DE56 4 C4
Milford Rd DE56 4 C2
Milford St DE1 10 C4
Mill Cl Borrowash DE72 13 E1
Findern DE65 14 B1
Mill Croft DE3 9 E2
Mill Hill DE24 17 E2
Mill La Belper DE56 3 D2
Derby DE74 9 E2
Mill Moor Cl DE73 16 C1
Mill St Belper DE56 3 D2
Derby DE1 10 C3
Milldale Ct DE56 3 D2
Milldale Rd DE21 12 C2
Millers Dale Cl DE56 3 E3
Millom Pl DE21 7 E1
Milton Rd DE65 9 E2
Milton St DE22 10 B2
Mimosa Cres DE23 15 F3
Minster Rd DE21 7 F1
Misterton Cl DE22 6 C1
Mitcham Wlk DE22 10 A3
Moira Cl DE21 12 A4
Molineux St DE23 11 D1
Monarch Dr DE21 8 B2
Moncrieff Cres DE21 12 A4
Mondello Dr DE24 17 E3
Monks Cl DE24 15 E2
Monmouth St DE21 11 E3
Monsal Dr DE21 12 C2
Montpelier DE22 6 B4
Montrose Cl DE24 15 F2
Monyash Cl DE21 12 A4
Monyash Way DE56 3 D3
Moor Dr DE24 17 D3
Moor End DE21 12 C3
Moor La Barrow u T DE73 18 A4
Derby DE24 16 B3
Kirk Langley DE6 9 D4
Little Eaton DE21 5 F1
Ockbrook DE72 13 E3
Moor Rd DE7 7 F3
Moor Rise DE56 5 E4
Moor St DE21 12 C3
Moore St DE23 11 D2
Moorfield Ave DE56 5 E4
Moorgate DE22 9 F3
Moorhead Ave DE24 16 C3
Moorhead Prim Sch DE24 16 C3
Moorland Rd DE3 9 E2
Moorpool Cres DE56 5 E4
Moorside Cres DE24 15 F2
Moorside La DE56 5 E4
Moorway DE21 7 F2
Moorway Croft DE23 15 D4
Moorway La DE23 15 D3
Moorways Sports Ctr
DE24 16 B3
Morden Gn DE22 10 A3
Morefern Dr DE21 7 F1
Morley Almshouses La DE7 8 A4
Morley Cl DE56 3 F3
Morley La
Breadsall DE7, DE21 7 F4
Little Eaton DE7, DE21 7 F4
Morley Prim Sch DE7 8 B4
Morley Rd DE21 8 B1
Morley St DE22 10 B3
Morlich Dr DE24 15 F3
Morningside Cl DE24 16 B2
Mornington Cres DE22 10 A3
Morpeth Gdns DE21 7 E1
Morrell Wood Dr DE56 3 E3
Mortimer St DE24 16 B4
Mosedale Cl DE24 16 C4
Moses La DE7 8 C3
Moss St DE22 10 C2
Mostyn Ave DE23 10 B1
Mottistone Cl DE24 17 E3
Moult Ave DE21 12 C2
Moulton Cl DE56 3 E3
Mount Pleasant Dr
Belper DE56 2 C3
Heage DE56 3 F4
Mountfield Way DE24 17 E2
Mountford Cl DE21 8 A1
Mowbray St DE24 16 B4
Moy Ave DE24 15 F1
Moyne Gdns DE73 19 D4
Muirfield Dr DE3 9 F1
Mulberry Cl DE56 3 D2
Mull Ct 9 DE24 15 E2
Mullberries Ct DE22 6 C2
Mullion Pl DE24 17 D3
Mundy Cl DE1 10 C3
Mundy St DE1 10 C3
Murray Park Com Sch DE3 9 F2
Murray Rd DE3 9 F2
Murray St DE24 16 C4
Muswell Rd DE22 9 F3
Myers Cl DE24 15 F2

Nailers Way DE56 3 E3
Nairn Ave DE21 11 E4
Nairn Cl DE24 15 E2
Namur Cl DE22 10 B2
Napier Cl DE3 9 F2
Napier St DE22 10 B3
Naseby Cl DE3 9 E2
Naseby Rd DE56 3 E2
Nearwood Dr DE21 7 F2
Neilson St DE24 16 C4
Nelson Cl DE3 9 F2
Nesfield Cl DE24 17 E4
Ness Wlk DE22 6 C2
Nether Cl DE56 4 C3
Nether La Hazelwood DE56 4 A4
Holbrook DE56 5 E3
Netherclose St DE23 11 D1
Netherside Dr DE73 17 D1
Netherwood Ct DE22 6 B2
Nettlefold Cres DE73 19 D1
Nevinson Ave DE23 15 E4
Nevinson Dr DE23 15 E4
Nevis Cl DE24 15 E1
New Breck Rd DE56 3 D2
New Inn La DE21 7 E4
New Mount Cl DE23 15 E3
New Rd Belper DE56 2 C2
Derby DE65 7 D1
Heage DE56 3 E4
Heage DE56 3 E4
Turnditch DE56 1 D2
New St Little Eaton DE21 7 E4
Ockbrook DE72 13 E2
New Zealand La DE56 4 C1
New Zealand Sq DE22 10 B3
Newark Rd DE21 7 E1
Newbold Ave DE72 13 E1
Newbold Cl DE73 16 C1
Newborough Rd DE24 17 E3
Newbridge Cres DE24 16 C2
Newbury St DE24 16 C4
Newchase Bsns Pk DE23 11 D1
Newdigate St DE23 16 A4
Newgate Cl DE73 17 D1
Newhaven Rd DE21 12 A3
Newlyn Dr DE23 15 F4
Newmarket Ct DE24 11 F1
Newmarket Dr DE24 16 C4
Newport Ct DE24 17 E3
Newquay Pl DE24 17 E3
Newstead Ave DE21 11 F3
Newton Cl DE56 3 E3
Newton's Wlk DE22 10 C4
Nicholas Cl DE21 12 C3
Nicola Gdns DE23 15 E2
Nidderdale Ct DE24 17 E3
Nightingale Inf Sch DE24 16 B4
Nightingale Jun Sch DE24 16 B4
Nightingale Rd DE24 16 B4
Noel St DE22 10 B3
Noel-Baker Com Sch
DE24 16 C2
Nook The Barrow u T DE73 18 A3
Holbrook DE56 5 E4
Norbury Cl DE22 6 C1
Norbury Cres DE23 15 E3
Norbury Ct DE22 6 B1
Norbury Way DE56 3 E3
Norfolk Gdns DE22 10 C4
Norfolk St DE23 11 D1
Norman Ave DE23 15 F4
Normanton Inf Sch DE23 15 F4
Normanton Jun Sch
DE23 15 F4
Normanton La DE23 15 D4
Normanton Village Inf Sch
DE23 15 F4
North Ave
Derby, Darley Abbey DE3 7 D2
Derby, Mickleover DE3 9 F1
North Cl DE65 9 F2
North La
Belper, Farnah Green DE56 2 B1
Belper, Milford DE56 4 C4
North Row DE22 7 D1
North St DE23 10 B1
Northacre Rd DE21 8 A1
Northfield Derby DE24 15 E2
Kilburn DE56 3 F1
Northmead Dr DE3 10 A2
Northumberland St DE23 10 C1
Northwood Ave DE21 11 F4
Norwich St DE21 11 F4
Norwood Cl DE22 10 A3
Nottingham Rd
Belper DE56 3 D2
Borrowash DE72 13 E1
Derby, Chaddesden DE21 11 F3
Derby, Spondon DE21 12 C2
Nun's St DE1 10 C3
Nunsfield Dr DE24 17 D4
Nursery Cl DE72 13 D1
Nutwood Cl DE22 7 D2

Oadby Rise DE23 15 F3
Oak Cl Derby DE72 6 C2
Duffield DE56 4 C1
Ockbrook DE72 13 E3
Oak Cres DE23 15 E4
Oak Dr Derby, Boulton DE24 17 D3
Derby, Mickleover DE65 9 F1
Oak Rd DE72 17 F2
Oak St DE23 11 D1
Oak Tree Ct DE72 13 E1
Oakham Cl DE21 7 E1
Oakhurst Cl DE56 2 B3
Oaklands Ave DE23 15 E3
Oakleigh Ave DE21 11 F3
Oakover Dr DE22 6 B1
Oakridge DE21 12 A4
Oaks The DE21 7 E4
Oakside Way DE21 8 A2
Oaktree Ave DE24 16 A4
Oakwood Cl DE65 15 E1
Oakwood District Ctr
DE21 8 A1
Oakwood Dr DE21 8 A1
Oakwood Inf Sch DE24 17 D3
Oakwood Jun Sch DE24 17 D3
Ockbrook Sch DE72 13 E3
Offerton Ave DE23 15 F4
Old Barn Cl DE21 7 E4
Old Chester Rd DE1 11 D4
Old Church La DE22 6 B3
Old Gate Ave DE72 19 F3
Old Hall Ave
Derby, Alvaston DE24 17 D4
Derby, Littleover DE23 10 A1
Duffield DE56 4 C2
Old Hall Mills Bsns Pk
DE21 7 E4
Old Hall Rd DE23 10 B1
Old Highcliff La DE56 1 D2
Old La Derby DE22 7 D1
Shottle DE56 1 D3
Old Mansfield Rd DE21 7 E1
Old Mill Cl DE56 4 C2
Old Rd DE56 3 F4
Old Vicarage Cl DE23 10 B1
Old Vicarage La DE22 6 B3
Old Vicarage Sch The DE22 7 D2
Oldbury Cl DE21 8 A1
Olive Gr DE21 11 F3
Olive St DE22 10 C2
Olivier St DE23 11 D1
Olton Rd DE3 9 E2
Onslow Rd DE3 9 F2
Opal Cl DE21 8 A1
Openwood Rd DE56 3 F2
Openwoodgate DE56 3 E2
Orchard Cl Belper DE56 5 D4
Derby DE23 15 E4
Elvaston DE24 17 E2
Ockbrook DE72 13 E2
Orchard Cotts DE56 4 C2
Orchard Ct DE21 12 C3
Orchard St DE3 9 E1
Orchard The DE56 3 D2
Orchard Way DE73 16 C1
Orchards The DE22 6 B2
Ordish Ave DE21 11 F3
Oregon Way DE21 12 B3
Orkney Cl DE24 15 E2
Ormskirk Rise DE21 12 C2
Osborne Rd DE23 11 E2
Osmaston Park Ind Est
DE24 16 C4
Osmaston Rd DE23 11 D1
Osprey Cl DE24 15 F1
Osterly Gn DE22 10 A3
Oswestry Cl DE21 8 A2
Otter St DE1 11 D4
Otterburn Dr DE22 6 B1
Oulton Cl DE24 16 B2
Outram Way DE24 15 F1
Oval Ct DE23 15 E4
Over La Belper DE56 3 F3
Hazelwood DE56 2 A1
Overdale Rd DE23 10 C1
Overstone Cl DE56 3 E2
Owlers La DE23 10 B1
Owlswick Cl DE23 15 D4
Oxenhope Cl DE23 14 C4
Oxford St DE21 12 C3
Oxwich Ct DE21 8 A1

Paddock Croft DE21 7 F1
Paddock The
Elvaston DE24 17 E2
Ockbrook DE72 13 E2
Padley Cl DE22 7 D3
Padstow Cl DE24 15 E2
Padstow Rd DE24 17 E3
Palatine Gr DE23 14 C4
Pall Mall DE21 7 F2
Palladium Dr DE23 15 D3
Palm Cl DE23 10 A1
Palmerston St DE23 10 C1
Pamela's Cl DE21 13 D3
Parade The DE3 9 E1
Parcel Terr DE22 10 B3
Pares Way DE72 13 E3
Park Cl DE21 7 D4
Park Cres DE56 3 F4
Park Dr DE23 10 B1
Park Farm Ctr DE22 6 B1
Park Farm Dr DE22 6 B1
Park Gr DE22 10 C4
Park Hill Dr DE23 15 F4
Park La
Derby, Allestree DE22 6 C2
Derby, Littleover DE23 10 B1
Weston-on-T DE72 19 F2
Park Leys Ct DE21 12 C2
Park Rd Belper DE56 3 D1
Derby, Mickleover DE3 9 E1
Derby, Spondon DE21 12 B3
Duffield DE56 4 B2
Heage DE56 3 F4
Park View Cl DE22 6 C2
Parker Ctr DE21 11 E4
Parker St DE1 10 C4
Parkfields Dr DE22 10 C4
Parklands Dr DE73 19 D4
Parkside DE56 3 F4
Parkside Rd DE21 12 A3
Parkstone Ct DE3 9 E1
Parkview DE21 7 E4
Parkway DE73 16 C1
Parliament Cl DE22 10 C2
Parliament St DE22 10 C2
Partridge Way DE3 10 A2
Pastures Ave DE23 14 C4
Pastures Hill DE23 15 D4

Pastures Hospl DE3 14 A4
Pastures The DE56 4 C2
Paterson Ave DE21 12 A3
Patmore Sq DE23 15 F4
Patten Ct DE24 16 A3
Pavilion Rd DE23 15 E4
Paxton Cl DE3 9 E1
Payne St DE22 10 B3
Peach St DE22 10 B3
Pear Tree Com Jun & Inf Schs DE23 16 A4
Pear Tree Cres DE23 16 A4
Pear Tree Ind Pk DE23 16 A4
Pear Tree St DE23 11 D1
Pear Tree Sta DE23 16 A4
Pearl Cl DE21 8 A1
Peartree Ct DE21 7 E1
Peartree Schs DE23 11 D1
Peckham Gdns DE22 10 A3
Peebles Cl DE24 15 F1
Peel St DE22 10 B3
Peers Cl DE21 8 A1
Peet St DE22 10 C2
Peggs Wlk DE23 15 F4
Pegwell Cl DE23 15 E4
Pelham St DE22 10 C2
Pembroke St DE21 11 E4
Penalton Cl DE24 16 C3
Pendennis Cl DE24 17 D3
Pendlebury Dr DE3 9 F1
Pendleside Way DE23 14 C4
Penge Rd DE22 10 A4
Penhaligan's Cl DE73 16 C1
Penine View DE56 3 F4
Penn St DE56 3 D2
Penny Long La DE22 10 C4
Pennycress Cl DE23 15 D4
Penrhyn Ave DE23 10 B1
Penrith Pl DE21 7 E1
Pentagon The DE21 11 E3
Pentewen Cl DE22 6 C1
Pentland Cl DE21 8 A1
Penzance Rd DE24 17 D3
Percy St DE22 10 C2
Peregrine Cl 3 DE24 15 E2
Perth Cl DE3 9 F2
Perth St DE21 7 E1
Peterborough St DE21 11 F4
Peterhouse Terr DE23 11 D1
Peterlee Pl DE24 17 D3
Petersham Dr DE24 17 E3
Peveril Ave DE72 13 E1
Peveril St DE24 16 B3
Pheasant Field Dr DE21 13 D3
Philips Croft DE56 4 C2
Pickering Rise DE21 7 E1
Pilgrims Way DE24 15 E2
Pilsley Cl DE56 3 E3
Pimlico DE22 10 A3
Pimm's Rd DE6 9 D4
Pinchom's Hill Rd DE56 3 D2
Pine Cl DE21 12 A2
Pinecroft Ct DE21 8 A1
Pinewood Rd DE56 2 C3
Pinfold The Belper DE56 3 E3
Elvaston DE72 17 F2
Pingle DE22 6 C2
Pingle Cres DE56 2 C3
Pingle La DE56 2 C3
Pingle The DE21 12 C2
Pintail Dr DE24 15 E2
Pit Close La DE73 17 D1
Plains La DE56 2 A2
Plantain Gdns DE23 15 E3
Plimsoll St DE22 10 B3
Plough Gate DE22 6 C1
Ploughfield Cl DE23 15 D3
Pole's Rd DE6 9 D4
Pollards Oaks DE72 13 E1
Pond Rd DE56 5 E4
Ponsonby Terr DE1 10 C3
Pontefract St DE24 16 B4
Pontypool Cl DE21 8 A1
Pool Cl DE24 17 E2
Poole St DE24 16 C3
Poplar Ave DE21 12 C3
Poplar Cl DE24 17 D4
Poplar Nook DE22 6 C2
Poplar Row DE22 7 D1
Poplars The DE22 6 C2
Porlock Ct DE21 8 A1
Port Way DE21, DE56 5 E3
Porter Rd DE23 10 C1
Porter's La Derby DE21 7 F2
Findern DE65 14 B1
Porthcawl Pl DE21 8 B1
Portland Cl DE3 9 E1
Portland St DE23 16 A4
Portman Chase DE24 15 E1
Portreath Dr DE22 6 C2
Portway Cl DE22 7 D2
Portway Inf & Jun Sch DE22 6 C2
Potter St DE21 12 B2
Pottery Cl DE56 3 E3
Pottery Prim Sch DE56 3 E2
Powell St DE23 10 C1
Poyser Ave DE21 12 A4
Prescot Cl DE3 9 E1
Prestbury Cl DE21 8 A1
Pride Park Stad (Derby FC) DE21 11 F2
Pride Parkway DE21 11 E2
Priestland Ave DE21 12 B2
Primary Cl DE56 3 D2
Prime Ind Est DE23 11 D1
Prime Ind Pk DE23 11 E1
Primrose Cl DE21 7 F2
Primrose Dr DE7 8 B4
Primula Way DE23 15 E2
Prince Charles Ave DE22 10 A3
Princes Dr DE23 10 A1
Princes St DE23 11 D1
Princess Dr DE72 13 D1
Priors Barn Cl DE72 13 E1
Priorway Ave DE72 13 E1
Priorway Gdns DE72 13 E1
Priory Cl DE73 19 D4
Pritchett Dr DE23 14 C4
Prospect Dr DE56 2 C1
Prospect Rd DE56 3 F1
Provident St DE23 11 D1
Pulborough Gdns DE23 15 D3
Pullman Rd DE21 11 F2
Putney Cl DE22 9 F3
Pybus St DE22 10 B3
Pykestone Cl DE21 7 F1
Pytchley Cl DE56 3 E2

Quantock Cl DE24 15 E1
Quarn Dr DE22 6 B2
Quarn Gdns DE1 10 C4
Quarn St DE1 10 C4
Quarn Way DE1 10 C3
Quarndon Hts DE22 6 B2
Quarndon View DE22 6 B1
Quarry Rd Belper DE56 2 C1
Morley DE7 8 A4
Queen Mary Ct DE1 10 C4
Queen St DE56 3 D2
Queen's Dr DE56 2 C3
Queens Dr DE23 10 B1
Queensferry Gdns DE24 16 C2
Queensland Cl DE3 9 F2
Queensway DE22 6 C1
Quick Hill Rd DE24 15 E1
Quillings Way DE72 13 E1
Quorn Rise DE23 15 F3

Rabown Ave DE23 15 E4
Racecourse Ind Est DE21 11 E4
Radbourne La DE22 9 F3
Radbourne St DE22 10 B3
Radcliffe Ave DE21 11 F4
Radcliffe Dr DE22 10 B2
Radford St DE24 16 C4
Radnor St DE21 11 E4
Radstock Gdns DE21 7 F1
Radstone Cl DE21 8 A1
Raglan Ave DE22 10 B3
Rainham Gdns DE24 17 D3
Rainier Dr DE21 12 A3
Raleigh St DE22 10 B3
Ramblers Dr DE21 8 B2
Ramsdean Cl DE21 11 E4
Ramshaw Way DE22 10 C2
Randolph Rd DE23 15 F4
Ranelagh Gdns DE22 10 A4
Rangemore Cl DE3 9 F2
Rannoch Cl
Derby, Allestree DE22 6 C2
Derby, Spondon DE21 12 C3
Ranworth Cl DE24 16 B2
Raven Oak Cl DE56 3 D2
Raven St DE22 10 C2
Ravenscourt Rd DE22 10 B3
Ravenscroft Dr DE21 11 F3
Ravensdale Inf & Jun Sch DE3 9 F2
Ravensdale Rd DE22 6 B2
Rawdon St DE23 10 C1
Rawlinson Ave DE23 16 A4
Rawson Gn DE56 3 F1
Raynesway DE21 12 A2
Raynesway Park Dr DE21 12 A1
Reader St DE21 12 C3
Rectory Farm Mews DE72 19 F2
Rectory La DE21 7 E3
Reculver Cl DE23 15 E4
Red La DE56 5 D3
Redbury Cl DE1 10 C2
Redcar Gdns DE21 7 E1
Redhill Prim Sch DE72 13 E3
Redland Cl DE24 15 F2
Redmires Dr DE73 17 D1
Redruth Pl DE24 17 E3
Redshaw St DE1 10 C4
Redstart Cl DE21 12 C3
Redwing Croft DE23 15 E4
Redwood Inf Sch DE24 15 F2
Redwood Jun Sch DE24 15 F2
Redwood Rd DE24 15 F2
Reeves Rd DE23 11 D1
Regency Cl DE23 15 E4
Reginald Rd N DE21 11 F4
Reginald Rd S DE21 11 F3
Reginald St DE23 11 D1
Regis Cl DE21 8 A1
Reigate Dr DE22 10 A4
Reigate Prim Sch DE22 9 F4
Renfrew St DE21 11 F4
Repton Ave DE23 10 B1
Retford Cl DE21 7 E1
Ribblesdale Cl DE22 6 B1
Richardson St DE22 10 B3
Richmond Ave DE72 15 E4
Richmond Dr DE56 4 B3
Richmond Rd
Derby, Chaddesden DE21 11 F3
Derby, Rose Hill DE23 11 D1
Riddings DE22 6 C2
Riddings St DE22 10 C2
Ridgeway DE73 19 D4
Ridgeway Ave DE23 15 E3
Ridgeway Inf Sch DE23 15 E3
Ridgewood Ct DE21 7 F1
Ridings The DE72 13 E3
Rigga La DE56 5 D1
Rigsby Ct DE3 9 E2
Rimsdale Cl DE24 15 F2
Ringwood Cl DE21 11 F4
Ripon Cres DE21 11 F4
Rise The DE22 6 C1
Rivenhall Cl DE23 14 C4
River View DE56 4 C4
Riverside Rd DE21 11 E2
Robin Croft Rd DE22 6 C2
Robin Rd DE1 10 C4
Robina Cl DE21 8 B2
Robinscross DE72 13 D1
Robinson Ind Est DE23 11 D1
Robson Cl DE24 17 D4
Rochester Cl DE24 17 D3
Rochley Cl DE21 7 F1
Rockbourne Cl DE24 17 E3
Rockhouse Rd DE24 17 D3
Rockingham Cl DE22 7 D2
Rodney Wlk DE23 14 C4
Rodsley Cres DE23 15 E3
Roe Farm La DE21 11 F4
Roe Wlk DE23 11 D1
Roehampton Dr DE22 10 A4
Roman Rd DE1 11 D4
Roman Way DE72 13 E1
Romsley Cl DE3 9 E2
Rona Cl DE24 15 F2
Ronald Cl DE23 14 C4
Roosevelt Ave DE21 12 A3
Rosamond's Ride DE23 15 E4
Rose Ave DE72 13 E1
Rose Farm Prim Sch DE21 11 F4
Rose Hill St DE23 11 D1
Roseberry Ct DE21 8 A1
Rosedale Ave DE24 17 D3
Roseheath Cl DE23 15 F3
Rosehill Inf Sch DE23 11 D2
Rosemary Dr DE24 17 D3
Rosemoor La DE21 8 A1
Rosemount Ct DE22 6 B2
Rosette Cl DE21 8 B2
Rosewood Cl DE24 17 E4
Ross Wlk DE21 7 F1
Rossington Dr DE23 14 C3
Rosslyn Gdns DE24 17 D3
Rothbury Pl DE21 7 F1
Rothesay Cl DE24 15 F2
Rothwell La DE56 3 D2
Rothwell Rd DE3 9 E2
Rough Heanor Rd DE3 10 A1
Roughton Cl DE3 14 B4
Rowan Cl
Derby, Cherrytree Hill DE21 12 A3
Derby, Sinfin DE24 15 E2
Rowan Park Cl DE23 15 E4
Rowditch Ave DE22 10 B2
Rowditch Pl DE22 10 B2
Rowena Cl DE24 16 C4
Rowland St DE24 16 C3
Rowley Gdns DE23 15 E4
Rowley La DE23 15 E4
Rowsley Ave DE23 15 E4
Roxburgh Ave DE21 11 F4
Royal Cl DE72 13 D1
Royal Gate DE56 3 E2
Royal Gr DE21 8 B2
Royal Hill Rd DE21 12 B3
Royal Sch for the Deaf DE22 10 B3
Roydon Cl DE3 9 E2
Royston Dr DE56 3 E3
Rudyard Ave DE21 12 C3
Ruffstone Cl DE56 5 E4
Rugby St DE24 11 F1
Rupert Rd DE21 12 A4
Rushcliffe Ave DE21 11 F3
Rushdale Ave DE23 15 E3
Rushup Cl DE22 7 D3
Ruskin Rd DE1 10 C4
Ruskin Way DE23 15 D4
Russell St DE24 11 E1
Russet Cl DE21 8 A1
Rutherford Dr DE21 7 F1
Rutland Ave DE72 13 E1
Rutland Dr DE3 9 F2
Rutland St DE23 11 D1
Ryal Cl DE72 13 E3
Ryan Cl DE24 15 F2
Rydal Cl DE22 6 C2
Rye Butts DE73 16 C1
Rye Cl DE21 7 F2
Ryedale Gdns DE23 15 E3
Ryegrass Cl DE56 3 E2
Ryegrass Rd DE21 8 B1
Rykneld Cl DE23 14 C3
Rykneld Dr DE23 14 C4
Rykneld Rd Derby DE23 14 C3
Findern DE23 14 C3
Rykneld Way DE23 14 C3
Rymill Dr DE21 7 F1

Sackville St DE23 15 F4
Saddleworth Wlk DE24 16 C2
Saffron Dr DE21 8 A1
St Agnes Ave DE22 6 B2
St Alban's RC Prim Sch DE21 11 F3
St Albans Rd DE22 10 B2
St Alkmund's Cl DE56 4 C2
St Alkmunds Way DE56 4 C2
St Andrews Specl Sch DE21 7 F1
St Andrews View DE21 7 F1
St Anne's Cl DE1 10 C3
St Augustine St DE23 10 C1
St Benedict RC Sch DE22 6 C1
St Bride's Wlk DE22 10 A3
St Chad's CE Inf Sch DE23 10 C2
St Chad's Rd DE23 10 C1
St Clare's Cl DE22 10 B1
St Clare's Specl Sch DE3 10 A1
St Cuthbert's Rd DE22 10 B2
St David's Cl DE22 10 B2
St Edmund's Cl DE22 6 C2
St Elizabeth's RC Prim Sch DE56 2 C3
St Francis Ley Ind Pk DE23 11 D1
St George's Pl DE56 2 C2
St George's RC Prim Sch DE23 15 E4
St Giles Rd DE23 10 C1
St Giles Specl Sch DE21 7 E1
St Hugh's Cl DE22 7 D1
St James' CE Jun Sch DE23 11 D2
St James Cl DE56 3 E2
St James' St DE23 11 D1
St John Fisher RC Prim Sch DE24 17 E4
St John's Ave DE21 12 A3
St John's CE Prim Sch DE56 3 D3
St John's Cl DE22 6 B2
St John's Dr DE21 12 A3
St John's Rd DE56 3 D2
St John's Terr DE1 10 C3
St Mark's Rd DE21 11 E3
St Martin's Specl Sch DE24 16 C4
St Mary's Cl DE24 17 D3
St Marys Wharf Rd DE1 11 D4
St Matthew's Wlk DE22 6 C1
St Mawes Cl DE22 6 B2
St Mellion Cl DE3 9 F1
St Michael's Cl DE56 5 E3
St Michaels Cl DE24 17 E4
St Michaels View DE24 17 E4
St Nicholas Cl DE22 6 B1
St Paul's Rd DE1 11 D4
St Peter's CE Jun Sch DE23 10 B1
St Peter's Cl DE56 2 C2
St Peter's Rd DE73 17 D1
St Peters Croft DE56 3 D2
St Quentin Cl DE22 10 B2
St Ronan's Ave DE56 4 C1
St Stephen's Cl DE23 15 E3
St Stephens Cl DE72 13 D1
St Swithin's Cl DE22 10 B2
St Thomas Rd DE23 11 D1
St Werburgh's CE Prim Sch DE21 12 B3
St Werburgh's View DE21 12 B3
St Wystan's Rd DE22 10 B2
Sale & Davys CE Prim Sch DE73 18 A3
Sale St DE23 11 D1
Sallywood Cl DE24 15 E1
Saltburn Cl DE21 7 E1
Samantha Ct DE21 8 A1
Sandalwood Cl DE24 17 E4
Sandbach Cl DE21 8 A1
Sandbed La DE56 3 E2
Sandcroft Rd DE21 12 C3
Sanderson Rd DE21 12 A3
Sandfield Cl DE21 12 A4
Sandgate Cl DE24 17 D3
Sandown Ave DE3 9 E2
Sandown Rd DE24 16 C4
Sandringham Dr DE21 12 C3
Sandringham Rd DE21 7 F1
Sandyhill Cl DE73 17 D1
Santolina Dr DE21 7 F1
Sapperton Cl DE23 15 E3
Saundersfoot Way DE21 8 B1
Saxondale Ave DE3 9 E2
Scarborough Rise DE21 7 E1
Scarcliffe Cl DE24 16 C2
Scarsdale Ave
Derby, Allestree DE23 6 B2
Derby, California DE23 10 B1
Scarsdale Rd DE56 4 C2
School La DE73 17 D1
Scothches The DE56 2 C3
Scott Dr DE56 3 F3
Scott St DE23 10 C1
Scropton Wlk DE24 16 C2
Seagrave Cl DE21 12 A4
Searl St DE1 10 C3
Seascale Cl DE21 7 E1
Seaton Cl DE3 9 E2
Second Ave DE73 19 D4
Sedgebrook Cl DE21 7 F1
Sedgefield Gn DE3 9 E1
Sefton Rd DE21 11 F3
Selborne St DE24 11 E1
Selkirk St DE21 11 F4
Selworthy Cl DE21 8 A1
Selwyn St DE22 10 B3
Serina Ave DE23 15 E4
Settlement The DE72 13 E3
Sevenoaks Ave DE22 9 F3
Severn St DE24 16 C4
Severnale Cl DE22 7 D3
Severnlands Dr DE24 17 E2
Seymour Cl DE22 10 B3
Shacklecross Cl DE72 13 E1
Shaftesbury Cres DE23 11 D1
Shaftesbury St DE23 11 D1
Shaftesbury St S DE23 11 D1
Shakespeare St DE24 16 A3
Shaldon Dr DE23 10 B1
Shalfleet Dr DE24 17 E3
Shamrock St DE23 10 C1
Shandwick Ct 14 DE24 15 E2
Shannon Cl DE23 15 E3
Shardlow Rd DE24 17 E3
Shaw La DE56 5 D4
Shaw St DE22 10 C3
Shaw's Yd DE56 5 F4
Shaws Gn DE22 10 C3
Shearwater Cl DE23 15 E4
Sheldon Ct DE24 16 C2
Shelford Cl DE3 9 E2
Shelley Dr DE24 16 A3
Shelmory Cl DE24 16 C3
Shelton Dr DE24 16 C2
Shelton Jun & Inf Sch DE24 16 B2
Shenington Way DE21 8 A1
Shepherd St DE23 10 B1
Sherbourne Dr DE56 3 E3
Sheridan St DE24 15 F3
Sherston Cl DE21 8 A1
Sherwin St DE22 10 C4
Sherwood Ave
Borrowash DE72 13 E1
Derby, Chaddesden DE21 11 F4
Derby, Littleover DE23 15 E3
Sherwood St DE22 10 C2
Shetland Cl DE21 11 E4
Shipley Wlk DE24 16 C2
Shireoaks DE56 2 B3
Shirley Rd DE21 7 F1
Shop Stones DE72 13 E3
Short Ave DE22 6 C3
Short Lands DE56 3 D2
Short Row DE56 2 C2
Short St DE56 3 D2
Shorwell Gdns DE24 17 E3
Shottle Wlk DE24 16 C2
Shrewsbury Cl DE21 8 B1
Shropshire Ave DE21 11 F4
Siddals La DE22 6 C2
Siddons St DE24 17 D4
Sidings The DE21 12 A2
Sidmouth Cl DE24 17 E4
Sidney Cl DE3 9 F2
Silver Hill Rd DE23 11 D1
Silver La DE21 17 F3
Silverburn Dr DE21 8 A1
Silverhill Prim Sch DE3 9 E2
Silverhill Rd DE21 12 C2
Silverton Dr DE24 15 E1
Silvey Gr DE21 12 B2
Simcoe Leys DE73 17 D1
Simpson St DE24 16 C3
Sims Ave DE1 10 C3
Sinclair Cl DE24 15 F2
Sinfin Ave DE24 16 B2
Sinfin Central Sta DE24 16 A3
Sinfin Com Sch DE24 15 F2
Sinfin Fields Cres DE24 16 B3
Sinfin La Barrow u T DE73 18 A3
Derby DE24 15 F2
Sinfin Moor La
Derby, Chellaston DE73 16 C1
Derby, Sinfin DE73 15 F2
Sinfin North Sta DE24 16 A3
Sinfin Prim Sch DE24 15 F3
Sir Frank Whittle Rd DE21 11 E4
Siskin Dr DE24 15 E2
Sister's La DE72 13 E3
Sitwell Cl DE21 12 B2
Sitwell St DE21 12 C2
Skiddaw Dr DE3 9 F1
Skipton Gn DE21 7 E1
Skylark Way DE24 15 E2
Slack La
Derby, Darley Abbey DE22 6 C1
Derby, New Zealand DE22 10 B3
Slaidburn Cl DE3 9 F1
Slaney Cl DE24 16 C4
Slater Ave DE22 10 C3
Sledmere Cl DE24 17 E4
Sleepy La DE73 19 E1
Slindon Croft DE24 17 E3
Sloane Rd DE22 10 A3
Small Meer Cl DE73 16 C1
Smalley Dr DE21 8 A2
Smisby Way DE24 16 C2
Smith Ave DE73 19 D1
Snake La DE56 4 C2
Snelsmoor La DE73 17 D1
Snelston Cres DE23 10 B1
Snowberry Ave DE56 3 D2
Society Pl DE23 11 D1
Solway Cl DE21 8 A1
Somerby Way DE21 7 F1
Somersal Cl DE24 16 C2
Somerset St DE21 11 E4
Somme Rd DE22 6 A2
South Ave
Derby, Chellaston DE73 16 C2
Derby, Darley Abbey DE23 7 D2
Derby, Littleover DE23 10 B1
Derby, Spondon DE21 12 C2
South Brae Cl DE23 15 E4
South Dr
Derby, Chellaston DE73 16 C2
Derby, Cherrytree Hill DE21 12 A3
Derby, Little Chester DE1 10 C4
Derby, Littleover DE3 10 A1
South St DE1 10 C3
Southcroft DE23 15 E2

Southdown Cl DE24 15 E1
Southgate Cl DE3 9 E2
Southgate Inf Sch DE24 16 C4
Southmead Way DE3 10 A2
Southwark Cl DE22 10 A3
Southwood House
Specl Sch DE56 5 E3
Southwood St DE24 16 C4
Sovereign Way DE21 8 B2
Sparrow Cl DE24 15 E2
Speedwell Cl DE21 8 B2
Spenbeck Dr DE22 7 D3
Spencer Ave Belper DE56 3 D2
Derby DE24 16 B2
Spencer Rd DE56 3 D2
Spencer St DE24 17 D4
Spindletree Dr DE21 7 F1
Spinners Way DE56 3 E3
Spinney Cl DE22 7 D1
Spinney Rd
Derby, Chaddesden DE21 11 F4
Derby, St Luke's DE22 10 C2
Spinney The Belper DE56 3 D3
Borrowash DE72 13 E1
Spondon Sta DE21 12 B2
Spoonley Wood Ct DE23 14 C4
Spring Cl DE56 2 C3
Spring Gdns DE21 11 F4
Spring Hollow DE56 4 B4
Spring St DE22 10 C2
Springdale Ct DE3 9 F1
Springfield DE23 10 A1
Springfield Dr DE56 4 B2
Springfield Prim Sch
DE21 12 B3
Springfield Rd
Derby, Chellaston DE73 16 C1
Derby, Cherrytree Hill DE21 12 A3
Springwood Dr DE21 8 A1
Springwood L Ctr DE21 8 A1
Square The
Derby, Darley Abbey DE3 7 D1
Derby, Mickleover DE3 9 E1
Squires Way DE23 15 D4
Stables St DE22 10 B3
Stadmoor Ct DE73 16 C1
Staines Cl DE3 9 E1
Staithes Wlk DE21 7 E1
Staker La DE3 14 B3
Stamford St DE24 16 B3
Stanage Gn DE3 9 F1
Stanhope Rd DE3 9 F2
Stanhope St DE23 11 D1
Stanier Way DE21 12 A2
Stanley Cl DE22 10 C4
Stanley Rd
Derby, Allenton DE24 16 C3
Derby, Cherrytree Hill DE21 12 A3
Stanley St DE22 10 B3
Stanstead Rd DE3 9 E2
Stanton Ave DE56 3 D2
Stanton St DE23 10 C1
Starcross Ct DE3 9 E2
Statham St DE22 10 C4
Station App DE56 4 C2
Station Cl DE73 16 C1
Station Rd
Borrowash DE72 13 D1
Breadsall DE21 7 F2
Derby, Chellaston DE73 16 C1
Derby, Mickleover DE74 9 E2
Derby, Spondon DE21 12 B2
Duffield DE56 4 C2
Little Eaton DE21 7 E4
Staunton Ave DE23 15 F3
Staveley Cl DE24 16 C2
Staverton Dr DE3 9 E2
Steeple Cl DE21 7 F1
Stenson Ave DE23 15 F3
Stenson Fields Prim
Com Sch DE24 15 E1
Stenson Rd
Derby, Littlover DE23, DE24 15 E2
Derby, Sinfin DE23, DE24 15 E2
Stepping Cl DE22 10 C3
Stepping La DE22 10 C3
Stevenage Cl DE24 16 C3
Stevenson Pl DE23 15 D4
Stewart Cl DE21 12 C3
Stiles Rd DE24 17 D4
Stirling Cl DE21 11 E4
Stockbrook Rd DE22 10 B2
Stockbrook St DE22 10 C2
Stocker Ave DE24 17 E4
Stoke Cl DE56 3 F3
Stone Cl DE21 12 C3
Stone Hill Rd DE23 10 C1
Stonebroom Wlk DE24 16 C2
Stonechat Cl DE3 10 A2
Stonesby Cl DE21 7 F1
Stonesdale Ct DE24 17 E3
Stoney Cross DE21 12 C2
Stoney Flatts Cres DE21 12 A4
Stoney La DE21 12 C3
Stony La DE56 5 E3
Stonyhurst Ct DE24 16 C2
Stoodley Pike Gdns DE22 6 B1
Stores Rd DE21 11 D4
Stornoway Cl DE24 15 E2
Stourport Dr DE73 17 D2
Stowmarket Dr DE21 11 E4
Stratford Rd DE21 7 E1
Strathaven Ct DE21 12 C3
Strathmore Ave DE24 17 D3
Streatham Rd DE22 10 A3
Stretton Cl DE3 9 E1
Stroma Cl DE24 15 F2
Strutt St Belper DE56 2 C2
Derby DE23 11 D1
Sturges La DE72 17 F2
Sudbury Cl DE1 10 C3
Sudbury St DE1 10 C3
Suffolk Ave DE21 11 F4
Summer Wood Ct DE23 15 E4
Summerbrook Ct DE22 10 C2
Sunart Cl DE24 15 F1
Sundew Cl DE21 12 C2
Sundown Ave DE23 15 E3
Sunningdale Ave DE21 12 B3
Sunny Bank Gdns DE56 2 C1
Sunny Gr DE21 12 A3
Sunny Hill DE56 4 C4
Sunnyhill Ave DE23 15 F3
Surbiton Cl DE22 10 A3
Surrey St DE22 10 B3
Sussex Cir DE21 11 F4
Sutherland Rd DE23 11 D1
Sutton Ave DE73 16 C2
Sutton Cl DE22 10 B3
Sutton Dr DE24 16 C2
Swaledale Ct DE24 17 E3
Swallow Cl DE3 10 A2
Swallowdale Rd DE24 15 E2
Swanmore Rd DE23 15 D4
Swanwick Gdns DE21 8 A1
Swarkestone Dr DE23 15 E3
Swarkestone Rd
Barrow u T DE73 18 A3
Derby DE73 18 C4
Swarkstone Rd DE73 18 A3
Swayfield Cl DE3 9 E2
Sweetbriar Cl DE24 17 D3
Swift Cl DE3 10 A2
Swinderby Dr DE21 8 A1
Swinney Bank DE56 3 D3
Swinney La DE56 3 D3
Sycamore Ave
Derby DE65 6 B2
Findern DE65 14 C1
Sydenham Rd DE22 10 A4

Taddington Cl DE21 11 F4
Taddington Rd DE21 7 F1
Talbot St DE1 10 C3
Talgarth Cl DE21 8 B1
Tamar Ave DE22 6 B2
Tamworth St DE56 4 C2
Tamworth Terr DE56 4 C2
Tansley Rise DE21 7 F1
Tants Meadow DE56 5 F3
Taplow Cl DE3 9 E1
Tarina Cl DE73 17 D1
Tasman Cl DE3 9 F2
Taunton Cl DE24 17 E4
Taverners Cres DE23 15 E4
Tavistock Cl DE24 15 E2
Tawny Way DE23 15 D4
Tay Cl DE24 15 E1
Tay Wlk DE22 6 C2
Taylor St DE24 11 F1
Tayside Cl DE24 15 E2
Tedworth Ave DE24 15 E1
Telford Cl DE3 9 F1
Templar Cl DE24 15 E2
Temple St DE23 11 D2
Tennessee Rd DE21 12 A4
Tennyson St DE24 16 B4
Terry Pl DE24 16 C4
Teviot Pl DE21 8 A1
Tewkesbury Cres DE21 11 E4
Thackeray St DE24 16 A3
Thames Cl DE22 9 F3
Thanet Dr DE24 17 D3
Thirlmere Ave DE22 6 C2
Thirsk Pl DE24 16 B4
Thistledown Cl DE22 7 D1
Thoresby Cl DE21 8 A1
Thorn Cl DE22 6 B2
Thorn St DE23 10 C1
Thorndike Ave DE24 17 D4
Thorndon Cl DE3 14 B4
Thorness Cl DE24 17 E3
Thornhill Rd
Derby, California DE22 10 B2
Derby, Littleover DE23 10 B1
Thorpe Dr DE3 9 F2
Thorpe Way DE56 3 D3
Thorpelands Dr DE22 6 C1
Three Gates DE56 2 C1
Thrushton Cl DE65 14 B1
Thruxton Cl DE24 17 E3
Thurlow Ct DE21 8 A1
Thurrows Way DE73 17 D1
Thurstone Furlong DE73 16 C1
Thyme Cl DE23 15 E2
Tiber Cl DE24 17 E3
Tickham Ave DE24 15 E1
Ticknall Wlk DE23 15 F3
Tideswell Rd DE21 7 F1
Tilbury Pl DE24 17 D3
Timbersbrook Cl DE21 8 A1
Timsbury Ct DE21 7 F1
Tintagel Cl DE23 11 D1
Tiree Cl DE24 15 F2
Tissington Dr DE21 8 A2
Tiverton Cl DE3 9 E2
Tivoli Gdns DE1 10 C4
Tobermory Way DE24 15 E2
Tomlinson Ind Est DE21 7 D1
Tonbridge Dr DE24 17 D3
Top Farm Ct DE56 5 F4
Top La DE56 1 E4
Top Manor Cl DE72 13 E3
Topley Gdns DE21 7 F1
Torridon Cl DE24 15 F2
Tower St DE24 16 B4
Towle Cl DE72 13 E1
Town St Duffield DE56 4 C2
Holbrook DE56 5 E3
Town The DE21 7 E4
Townsend Gr DE73 17 D1
Trafford Way DE23 15 E4
Tredegar Dr DE21 8 A1
Trefoil Ct DE23 15 D4
Tregaron Cl DE21 8 B1
Tregony Way DE24 15 E2
Trent Bridge Ct DE23 15 E4
Trent Cl DE65 15 E1
Trent Dr DE23 15 E3
Trent La Melbourne DE73 19 E1
Weston-on-T DE72 19 F2
Trent Rise DE21 12 C2
Trent St DE24 17 D4
Trenton Green Dr DE21 12 A3
Trenton Grn DE21 12 A3
Tresillian Cl DE22 6 C1
Treveris Cl DE21 12 C2
Troon Cl DE23 15 D4
Trowbridge Cl DE21 7 F1
Trowels La DE22 10 B2
Truro Cres DE21 11 F4
Trusley Gdns DE23 15 E3
Tudor Field Cl DE73 17 D1
Tudor Rd DE21 12 A3
Tufnell Gdns DE22 10 A4
Tulla Cl DE24 15 F1
Turnditch CE Prim Sch
DE56 1 D1
Turner St DE24 16 C3
Tuxford Cl DE21 8 A1
Twickenham Dr DE22 10 A3
Twin Oaks Cl DE23 14 C4
Twyford Rd DE73 18 A3
Tyndale Chase DE24 15 E1

Uffa Magna DE3 9 E1
Ullswater Cl DE21 7 E1
Ullswater Dr DE21 12 C3
Underhill Ave DE23 15 F4
Underhill Cl DE23 15 F3
Univ of Derby DE22 6 B1
Upchurch Cl DE3 9 E2
Uplands Ave DE23 15 E3
Uplands Gdns DE23 10 C1
Upper Bainbridge St
DE23 11 D2
Upper Boundary Rd DE22 10 C2
Upper Dale Rd DE23 10 C1
Upper Hall Cl DE56 5 E3
Upper Hollow DE23 10 B1
Uppermoor Rd DE24 16 C3
Uttoxeter New Rd DE22 10 B2
Uttoxeter Old Rd DE22 10 C3
Uttoxeter Rd DE65 9 F1

Vale Mills DE22 10 C2
Valerie Rd DE72 19 F4
Valley Rd
Derby, Cherrytree Hill
DE21 12 A3
Derby, Littleover DE23 10 B1
Valley View DE56 3 D1
Vancouver Ave DE21 12 B2
Varley St DE24 16 B3
Vauxhall Ave DE22 10 A4
Verbena Dr DE23 15 E2
Vermont Dr DE21 12 B3
Vernon Dr DE21 12 C2
Vernon St DE1 10 C3
Vernongate DE1 10 C3
Vestry Rd DE21 7 F2
Vetchfield Cl DE24 15 F1
Vicarage Ave DE23 10 C1
Vicarage Cl DE56 3 D2
Vicarage Ct DE3 9 E1
Vicarage Dr DE21 12 A4
Vicarage La Duffield DE56 4 C2
Little Eaton DE21 7 E4
Vicarage Rd Belper DE56 4 C4
Derby, Chellaston DE73 16 C1
Derby, Mickleover DE3 9 E1
Vicarwood Ave Derby DE22 6 C1
Holbrook DE56 5 E4
Victor Ave DE22 10 C4
Victoria Ave DE72 13 D1
Victoria Cl DE3 9 F2
Victory Rd DE24 16 A3
Village Com Sch DE23 15 F4
Village Ct DE56 4 C2
Village St DE23 15 F4
Vincent Ave DE21 12 C2
Vincent St DE23 10 C1
Vine Cl DE23 15 D4
Viola Cl DE21 8 B2
Violet St DE23 10 C1
Vivian St DE1 11 D4
Vulcan St DE23 11 D1

Wade Ave DE23 10 B1
Wade Dr DE3 9 F1
Wade St DE23 10 B1
Wadebridge Gr DE24 17 E3
Wakami Cres DE73 17 D2
Walbrook Rd DE23 10 C1
Walcote Cl DE56 3 E3
Waldene Dr DE24 17 D3
Waldorf Ave DE24 17 D4
Waldorf Cl DE24 17 D4
Wallace St DE22 10 B3
Wallfields Cl DE65 14 B1
Walnut Ave DE24 17 D4
Walnut Cl
Barrow u T DE73 18 A3
Derby DE73 19 D4
Walnut Rd DE56 3 D2
Walnut St DE24 16 B4
Walpole St DE21 11 E3
Walsham Ct DE21 7 E1
Walter Evans CE Prim Sch
DE22 6 C1
Walter St DE1 10 C4
Waltham Ave DE24 15 F2
Walthamstow Dr DE22 10 A3
Walton Ave DE24 16 C2
Walton Dr DE23 15 F4
Walton Rd DE21 11 F3
Wansfell Cl DE3 9 F1
Ward St DE22 10 C2
Ward's La
King's Newton DE73 19 D1
Melbourne DE73 18 C2
Wardlow Ave DE21 12 A4
Warner St
Derby, Mickleover DE3 9 E1
Derby, St Luke's DE22 10 C2
Warren St DE24 16 C4
Warrendale Ct DE73 17 D1
Warwick Ave DE23 10 B1
Warwick Gdns DE56 3 E3
Warwick St DE24 11 E1
Washington Ave DE21 12 A3
Water Meadows The DE73 18 B3
Waterford Dr DE21 12 A2
Watergo La DE23 14 C4
Watering La DE56 5 E3
Watermeadow Rd DE24 17 D3
Waterside Cl DE22 7 D1
Watson St Derby DE1 10 C3
Derby DE1 10 C4
Watten Cl DE24 15 F1
Waveney Cl DE22 7 D3
Waverley St DE24 16 B4
Wayfaring Rd DE21 8 A1
Wayzgoose Dr DE21 11 E3
Weavers Cl Belper DE56 3 E3
Borrowash DE72 13 E1
Weavers Gn DE3 9 E1
Weirfield Rd DE22 7 D1
Welbeck Gr DE22 6 B2
Well La DE56 4 C4
Welland Cl DE3 9 E2
Wellesley Ave DE23 15 E4
Wellington Ct DE56 2 C2
Wells Ct DE23 14 C4
Wells Rd DE3 9 F1
Welney Cl DE3 14 B4
Welshpool Rd DE21 7 E1
Welwyn Ave
Derby, Allestree DE24 6 B2
Derby, Alleton DE24 16 C2
Wembley Gdns DE22 10 A3
Wendover Cl DE3 9 E1
Wenlock Cl DE3 9 F1
Wensley Dr DE21 12 C2
Wensleydale Wlk DE24 17 E4
Wentworth Cl DE3 9 F1
Werburgh Cl DE21 12 B2
Werburgh St DE22 10 C2
Wesley La DE72 13 E3
Wesley Rd DE24 17 D3
Wessington Mews DE22 6 C1
West Ave DE73 16 C2
West Bank Ave DE22 10 C4
West Bank Cl DE22 10 C4
West Bank Rd DE22 6 C3
West Cl DE22 6 C1
West Croft Ave DE23 15 E3
West Dr DE3 9 E1
West Gr DE24 16 B3
West Lawn DE65 14 B1
West Park Com Sch DE21 12 B3
West Park Rd DE22 10 C4
West Rd DE21 12 B3
West Row DE22 7 D1
West Service Rd DE21 12 A2
West View Ave DE23 15 D4
Westbourne Pk DE22 9 F4
Westbury Gdns DE56 3 E3
Westbury St DE22 10 C2
Westdene Ave DE24 16 B3
Western Rd
Derby, Mickleover DE3 9 F1
Derby, Rose Hill DE23 11 D2
Westgreen Ave DE24 16 B3
Westhall Rd DE3 9 E2
Westleigh Ave DE22 10 B3
Westley Cres DE21 5 E1
Westminster St DE24 16 C4
Westmorland Cl DE21 11 E3
Weston Park Ave DE24 16 C2
Weston Park Gdns DE24 16 B2
Weston Rd DE72 19 F3
Weston Rise DE73 19 D4
Weston-on-Trent
Parochial Prim Sch
DE72 19 F2
Westwood Dr DE24 16 B3
Wetherby Rd DE24 16 C4
Weyacres DE72 13 E1
Wharfedale Cl DE22 7 D2
Wheatcroft Way DE21 7 E1
Wheatland Cl DE24 15 E1
Wheatsheaf Cl DE21 8 B1
Wheeldon Ave Belper DE56 3 D2
Derby DE22 10 C4
Whenby Cl DE3 9 E1
Whernside Cl DE24 17 E3
Whilton Ct DE56 3 E2
Whinbush Ave DE24 16 C3
Whiston St DE23 11 D1
Whitaker Gdns DE23 10 C1
Whitaker Rd DE23 10 C1
Whitaker St DE23 11 D1
Whitby Ave DE21 7 E1
White Hart Yd DE56 5 F4
White La DE56 1 E2
White St DE22 10 C4
Whitecross Gdns DE1 10 C4
Whitecross St DE1 10 C3
Whitehouse Cl DE24 16 B2
Whitehouse Rise DE56 2 C3
Whitehurst St DE24 16 B4
Whitemoor Hall DE56 3 E3
Whitemoor La DE56 3 E3
Whiteway DE22 6 C1
Whitewell Gdns DE24 17 E3
Whitewells La DE56 2 B4
Whitmore Rd DE21 11 F3
Whitstable Cl DE23 15 E4
Whittaker La DE21 5 E1
Whittington St DE24 16 B3
Whittlebury Dr DE23 14 C4
Whyteleafe Gr DE21 8 A1
Wickersley Cl DE22 6 C1
Wicksteed Cl DE56 3 E3
Widdybank Cl DE22 6 B1
Wigmore Cl DE3 9 E2
Wild St DE22 10 B3
Wilderbrook La DE56 2 A4
Wilders Lea Ct DE56 3 D1
Wildsmith St DE24 17 D4
Wilfred St DE23 11 D1
Wilkins Dr DE24 16 C4
Willesden Ave DE22 10 A4
Willetts Rd DE21 12 A4
William Gilbert Endowed
Prim Sch DE56 4 C2
William St Belper DE56 2 C2
Derby DE1 10 C3
Willn St DE23 10 C1
Willow Cl DE72 6 C1
Willow Croft DE24 17 E2
Willow Farm Ct DE65 14 B1
Willow Gr DE56 3 D1
Willowbrook Grange
DE73 17 D1
Willowcroft Rd DE21 12 C2
Willowherb Cl DE24 15 F1
Willowsend Cl DE65 14 B1
Willson Ave DE23 15 E4
Willson Rd DE23 15 E4
Wilmington Ave DE24 17 D3
Wilmore Rd DE24 16 A3
Wilmorton Prim Sch DE24 11 F1
Wilmorton Tertiary Coll
DE24 11 F1
Wilmot Ave Derby DE21 11 F3
Weston-on-T DE72 19 F3
Wilmot Rd DE56 3 D2
Wilmslow Dr DE21 8 A1
Wilson Cl DE3 14 B4
Wilson Rd DE21 11 F4
Wilsthorpe Rd DE21 12 A4
Wilton Cl DE24 15 E1
Wiltshire Rd DE21 11 F4
Wimbledon Rd DE22 10 A4
Wimbourne Cl DE73 17 D1
Wimpole Gdns DE22 10 A3
Wincanton Cl DE24 11 E1
Winchcombe Way DE21 8 A1
Windermere Cres DE22 6 C2
Windermere Dr DE21 12 C3
Windley Cres DE22 6 C1
Windley La Shottle DE56 1 D3
Turnditch DE56 1 D1
Windmill Cl Elvaston DE24 17 E2
Ockbrook DE72 13 E3
Windmill Hill La DE22 10 B3
Windmill La DE56 3 D2
Windmill Rise DE56 3 D3
Windmill View DE56 3 F4
Windrush Cl DE22 7 D3
Windsor Ave DE73 15 D4
Windsor Cl DE72 13 E1
Windsor Ct DE3 9 E1
Windsor Dr DE21 13 D3
Windy La DE21 5 E1
Wingerworth Park Rd
DE21 12 C3
Wingfield Dr DE21 7 F1
Winslow Grn DE21 12 B3
Winster Cl DE56 3 D3
Winster Rd DE21 7 F1
Wintergreen Dr DE23 14 C3
Wirksworth Rd
Duffield DE56 4 B2
Shottle DE56 1 E2
Windley DE56 1 E2
Wisgreaves Rd DE24 16 C4
Witham Dr DE23 15 E3
Witney Cl DE24 16 B4
Woburn Pl DE22 10 A3
Wolfa St DE22 10 C2
Wollaton Rd DE21 11 F4
Wollaton Rd S DE21 7 F1
Wolverley Grange DE24 17 E3
Wood Croft DE23 15 E4
Wood La DE56 4 C4
Wood Rd
Derby, Chaddesden DE21 12 A4
Derby, Oakwood DE21 7 F1
Derby, Spondon DE21 13 D3
Woodale Cl DE23 14 C3
Woodbeck Ct DE21 8 A1
Woodbridge Cl DE73 16 C1
Woodchester Dr DE24 17 E3
Woodcote Way DE23 15 D4

Woodfall La DE56 .... 4 A1
Woodford Rd DE22 .... 10 A4
Woodgate Dr DE73 .... 17 D1
Woodhall Dr DE23 .... 14 C4
Woodhouse Rd DE56 .... 5 F4
Woodhurst Cl DE21 .... 11 E4
Woodland Ave DE72 .... 13 E1
Woodland Rd DE22 .... 10 C4
Woodlands Ave DE24 .... 16 C2
Woodlands Cl DE21 .... 7 D4
Woodlands Com Sch DE22 .... 6 B2
Woodlands La Derby DE73 .... 19 D4
   Quarndon DE22 .... 6 B3

Woodlands Rd DE22 .... 6 C3
Woodlands Yd DE73 .... 19 D4
Woodlea Gr DE21 .... 7 E4
Woodminton Dr DE73 .... 16 C2
Woodrising Cl DE21 .... 8 A2
Woodroffe Wlk DE23 .... 15 F4
Woodshop La DE73 .... 18 B3
Woodside Dr DE22 .... 7 D2
Woodsorrel Dr DE21 .... 8 A2
Woodstock Cl DE22 .... 6 B2
Woodthorpe Ave
   Derby, Allenton DE24 .... 16 C2
   Derby, Chaddesden DE21 .... 11 F3

Woodwards Cl DE72 .... 13 E1
Woolrych St DE23 .... 10 C1
Worcester Cres DE21 .... 11 F4
Wordsworth Ave DE24 .... 15 F3
Wordsworth Dr DE24 .... 16 A3
Wragley Way DE24 .... 15 E1
Wren Park Cl Belper DE56 .... 2 B3
   Findern DE65 .... 14 B1
Wren Park Prim Sch DE3 .... 10 A1
Wretham Cl DE3 .... 14 B4
Wroxham Cl DE24 .... 16 B2
Wyaston Cl DE22 .... 6 C1
Wye St DE24 .... 17 D4

Wyndham St DE24 .... 17 D4
Wynton Ave DE24 .... 16 C4
Wyver La DE56 .... 2 C4
Wyvern Way DE21 .... 12 A2

Yardley Way DE56 .... 3 E2
Yarrow Cl DE24 .... 15 F1
Yates St DE23 .... 11 D1
Yeovil Cl DE24 .... 17 E4
Yew Tree Ave DE72 .... 13 E3
Yew Tree La DE72 .... 17 F2
Yewdale Gr DE21 .... 8 B2
Yews Cl DE73 .... 17 D1

Yewtree Cl DE24 .... 17 E4
York Rd DE21 .... 11 F4
York St DE1 .... 10 C3
Youlgreave Cl DE21 .... 7 F1
Young St DE23 .... 10 C1
Ypres Rd DE22 .... 6 B1

Zetland Cres DE24 .... 15 E1

Ordnance Survey / Philip's Street Atlases

Colour Street Atlases
Hardback, spiral and pocket

- Berkshire
- Buckinghamshire
- Cheshire
- Derbyshire
- Derby and Belper *(paperback)*
- Durham
- North Hampshire
- South Hampshire
- Hertfordshire
- East Kent
- West Kent
- Lancashire
- Greater Manchester
- Merseyside
- Northwich, Winsford, Middlewich *(paperback)*
- Oxfordshire
- Peak District Towns *(paperback)*
- Surrey
- East Sussex

- West Sussex
- Tyne and Wear
- Warrington, Widnes, Runcorn *(paperback)*
- South Yorkshire
- West Yorkshire

Black and White Street Atlases
Hardback, spiral and pocket

- Bristol and Avon
- Cardiff, Swansea and Glamorgan
- Edinburgh & East Central Scotland
- East Essex
- West Essex
- Glasgow & West Central Scotland
- Nottinghamshire
- Staffordshire *(colour August 1998)*
- Warwickshire *(hardback only)*

Street Atlases on CD-ROM
- Interactive Street Atlas Berkshire
- Interactive Street Atlas Hertfordshire

Ordnance Survey Road Atlases

- Ordnance Survey Motoring Atlas Britain
- Ordnance Survey Superscale Atlas

The publications are available from all good bookshops. You can also order direct from the publisher by phoning the Customer Order Line on 01933 443863 from 9am to 5pm. Leave a message on the answering machine outside office hours.

Digital Data

The exceptionally high-quality mapping found in this book is available as digital data in TIFF format, which is easily convertible to other bit-mapped (raster) image formats.

The index is also available in digital form as a standard database table. It contains all the details found in the printed index together with the National Grid reference for the map square in which each entry is named and feature codes for places of interest in eight categories such as education and health.

For further information and to discuss your requirements, please contact the Ordnance Survey Solutions Centre on 01703 792929.